Extraordinary praise for
The Green Boat

"Mary Pipher spares us moral sermons and apocalyptic scenarios. Instead she shares her own journey. So we learn with her how to survive despair, how to feed the heart with beauty and the company of others, how to find balance together in the face of uncertainty and even moments of failure."

—Joanna Macy, coauthor of *Active Hope:*
How to Face the Mess We're in Without Going Crazy

"Mary Pipher has been our wise and steadfast guide through the worlds of adolescence, aging, and how families can teach humane values in a culture where everything is for sale. Now she's tackling the hardest question—how we can get past denial to reverse the human-caused climate change that jeopardizes the habitability of the world. As we'd expect, she does it thoughtfully, passionately, and ultimately with hope."

—Paul Loeb, author of *Soul of a Citizen*

"You should be concerned about the many devastating horrors we still inflict on our planet. But if you feel worried or hopeless, Mary Pipher has an insightful, friendly, and intimate new book that will help. With stories of local, mature activism, *The Green Boat* takes you through disturbing feelings about the future to a sense of hope. It's the book I've been waiting for, intelligently addressing the emotional issues involved without guilt and blame."

—Thomas Moore, author of *Cure of the Soul*

"Take a courageous, moving, and inspiring journey aboard this green boat. Discover how hopefulness and empowerment and joy grow, and how to pass honorably through heartache to the vast love that connects us all."

—Jack Kornfield, author of *A Path with Heart*

"Mary Pipher has a genius for illuminating in plain and poetic language the fundamental challenges we face in our complex and often overwhelming world. She maps out how we should wrestle with the realities of climate change and then shows us practical ways to both savor and help serve our planet."

—Daniel J. Siegel, MD, author of *Mindsight* and *The Developing Mind*

"This book is filled with wisdom, compassion, and the reminder that we are all still tuned to relationship. It personifies the hope and solidarity that comes from action, reminds us that one of our most effective skills is sticking together, and is a fantastic revelation of the big tent that we can be in."

—Peter Forbes, senior advisor, Center for Whole Communities, and author of *Our Land, Ourselves*

"With penetrating psychological wisdom and great heart, Mary Pipher invites us on a journey of deepening awareness that can save our planet."

—Tara Brach, author of *Radical Acceptance* and *True Refuge*

"Reading this book gave me the stirring hope that there are many of us who know that the farther shore is reachable from here. It is going on my 'hoper' shelf with a few other keystone books."

—Julia Alvarez, author of *Something to Declare*

Also by Mary Pipher

THE
Green Boat

*Reviving Ourselves in
Our Capsized Culture*

Mary Pipher

RIVERHEAD BOOKS

New York

RIVERHEAD BOOKS
Published by the Penguin Group
Penguin Group (USA) Inc.
375 Hudson Street, New York, New York 10014, USA

USA | Canada | UK | Ireland | Australia | New Zealand | India | South Africa | China

Penguin Books Ltd., Registered Offices: 80 Strand, London WC2R 0RL, England
For more information about the Penguin Group, visit penguin.com.

First Riverhead trade paperback edition: June 2013

Library of Congress Cataloging-in-Publication Data
Pipher, Mary Bray.
The green boat : reviving ourselves in our capsized culture / Mary Pipher.
p. cm.
ISBN 978-1-59448-585-5
1. Social change—Psychological aspects.   2. Social problems—Psychological aspects.
3. Culture shock.   4. Adjustment (Psychology)   I. Title.
HM831.P57 2013
303.4—dc23
2012043406

PRINTED IN THE UNITED STATES OF AMERICA

10 9 8 7 6 5 4 3 2 1

The publisher does not have any control over and does not assume any responsibility for author
or third-party websites or their content.

ALWAYS LEARNING   PEARSON

Dedicated to Susan Lee Cohen and Jane Isay,
who have been on board since the beginning.

Take this sinking boat and point it home.

We've still got time.

GLEN HANSARD

CONTENTS

RESILIENT COPING

THE TRANSCENDENT RESPONSE

INTRODUCTION

Humanity appears to be rapidly approaching
the breaking point. And there are two possible
outcomes: breakdown or breakthrough.

PETER RUSSELL

I began this book in the summer of 2010 at a time when the
world seemed almost too complicated and frightening for
me to manage emotionally. When I listened to the call of a
meadowlark or walked around the lake near my home, I was
serene. When I played hide-and-seek outdoors at dusk with
my grandchildren, I was happy, albeit mosquito bitten. But
when I turned on the news or read about the environment,
war, and the daily global injustices, I felt like jumping out of
my skin.

I sensed that many people felt this way. For example, most
of my news-junkie friends no longer read the news. And people who had once loved intense political conversations avoided
any talk about national or international affairs. People were
rushed, stressed, and edgy. Everyone looked tired. We were all
confused about what was going on and about how to fix it.

This book emerged from my attempt to understand myself
and the people around me. I wrote it for the same reasons I
wrote *Reviving Ophelia*. I sensed that individuals were struggling to deal with cultural problems. They felt alone, hopeless,

and uniquely damaged and they didn't realize that almost all of us felt that way.

~~~~~~~

Our individual anguish reflects enormous, systemic problems. On a global level, almost all major systems are breaking down. The problems include, but are not limited to: global climate change, drought and famine, overpopulation, diminishing resources, peak oil, the sixth great extinction of species, financial panic, and the specter of war. Indeed, sometimes it seems as if all that is holding our planet together is money-colored duct tape.

Scientist Will Steffen calls all these interconnected changes the Great Acceleration. While no one term encompasses the totality of what we are dealing with, Steffen's phrase reflects the tsunami of urgent and life-threatening planetary changes. Sometimes I'll refer to our problems as the "global storm." One definition of storm is "a violent disturbance of our atmosphere." That is exactly what we are navigating, literally and figuratively.

Our problems are made even more alarming by our inability to face them. Actually, that is our main problem. When a ship is sinking, pretending it isn't happening only intensifies the catastrophe. In fact, anytime we humans disconnect from reality, we enter individually and collectively what could be called a psychotic state.

Part of what makes our situation so surreal is that we don't know how to categorize it, we can't agree what caused it, and not everyone even believes we are in a crisis. We don't know how much time we have to react but we suspect that matters are urgent. And we don't talk about it, much less make plans to deal with it. As a species we are engaged in suicidal behavior that we cannot even discuss.

Of course people avoid facing problems they have no idea how to solve. All of us tune out information that seems unbearable. Yet our denial, while understandable and sometimes even useful, keeps us from grasping what we are up against and from talking about it, and it prevents us from responding adaptively to the situation around us.

The world has changed a great deal, but our basic homo sapiens minds and bodies have not changed since the Neolithic Era. In our twenty-first century, we humans are struggling unsuccessfully to cope with a world that challenges our basic physical, emotional, and cultural systems of resilience. We are in over our heads, and at some level, all of us are looking for a life buoy.

The Trauma-to-Transcendence Cycle

In *The Green Boat*, I explore a process that allows us to face the situation and cope with it in a resilient manner. It is within our power to make our lives less stressful and more joyful. This trauma-to-transcendence cycle allows us to once again be present and focused, to stay calm and balanced, and to attend to the world around us with great love. Of course we hope that our personal transformation leads to positive changes in the world, but without question it will change us.

Our reaction to overwhelming stress is trauma. At first, we simply are too stunned to respond. But gradually, healthy humans sort themselves out and find adaptive ways to deal with reality. This process requires us to face the truth, feel the pain of that experience, and ultimately transform that pain into action and authenticity. As we move through this cycle, we can acquire the skills we need to overcome our sense of doom and discover our own capacities for transcendent coping. By this I mean that we can find deep within ourselves new strength, deeper courage, and an enriched capacity to love the world. This cycle is not easy, but it is really the only sensible way to proceed in the current moment. And it gives us hope.

Abraham Maslow, the humanistic psychologist, is famous for his theory of a hierarchy of needs. He argues that humans first satisfy their most basic of needs—for water, food, and shelter—before they aspire to less tangible goals, such as love or respect. I have great regard for Maslow, but I have always felt his hierarchy was simplistic and that it misjudged the nature of human motivation. I would argue that our most basic needs are hope and love. We can be happy when we are cold or hungry, but we cannot be happy when we feel alone and without hope.

Neuroscientists have discovered that the human mind functions best when it acts as if there is hope and organizes itself to make good things happen. We can never fully know the significance and impact of our individual actions, but we can behave as though our actions have significance. That will create only good on earth and will allow us to function in a sane and intelligent way.

In his book *Steps to an Ecology of Mind*, Gregory Bateson

writes, "The unit of survival is the organism and its environment." We cannot protect our inner life unless we protect our outer life. The external is not so external after all. The only way we can be healthy as individuals is to create healthy environments around us. We are all mixed up together; our survival is contingent on the survival of other living beings.

These are not the times for tepid responses. We'll explore a new healthy normal, which is defined by awareness, engagement, passion, and balance. For me, balance means that the pain of facing reality is not more than the joys of connecting to the beauty of the world. One of the ways to achieve this kind of emotional balance is by participating in actions that help, especially with other like-minded people.

Throughout this book, I'll tell the story of our Coalition to Stop the Keystone XL Pipeline. Forming that coalition with my Nebraska friends was one of my primary coping devices and helped all of us deal with our anger and despair. I hope our story can serve as an example of resilient coping and perhaps even a transcendent response.

Just days before the election in the fall of 2012, Hurricane Sandy devastated coastal communities along the Atlantic from Cuba to New England. Like most Americans, I watched with horror as the lights went out and the floodwaters rose on the East Coast and in the Upper Midwest.

I knew that Sandy was no more a "natural disaster" than September 11 had been. The hurricane's size and strength were partly the results of melting polar ice caps, rising sea levels, and warmer seawater temperatures. And these tragic changes were caused by human-made problems. The old days were over. Almost everyone could see that.

Hurricane Sandy's effects were immediate: thousands of people were unable to go to work or school, many were left homeless, without heat, lights, or fuel. Most significantly, in terms of effecting cultural change, this event crashed into our country's pocketbook. Wall Street shut down for two days, the longest weather-related closing since 1888. Experts estimated that Sandy's costs, including crop damage, might exceed $75 billion.

This storm was almost certainly what's known as a climate signal, which is a weather phenomenon that can be explained only by taking into account new weather patterns attributable to global climate change.

It may also have signaled a cultural turning. Ideology, misinformation, and the psychological defense systems that have kept many Americans from accepting the reality of global climate change will hold for only so long. It is hard to deny impending climate catastrophes when one is up to one's waist in muddy salt water. Not surprisingly, it is the most practical among us who come out of denial first: the insurance company employees, the mass transit engineers, the mayors of coastal towns, and the builders. They must wake up in order to do their jobs.

As terrible as Sandy was, and I do not wish to minimize anyone's suffering, it also may have given us a culture-changing teachable moment. Overnight the great unmentionable, global climate change, became mentionable, not only by environmentalists, but by the media and by mainstream political leaders. I was heartened by New York City mayor Michael Bloomberg's endorsement of President Obama in which he specifically mentioned the need for a president who will deal with climate change. Then, in President Obama's post reelection speech, he told listeners, "We want our children to live in an America that isn't threatened by the destructive power of a warming planet."

This breaking of the silence surrounding global climate change gives me hope that, at last, we as a society might have a conversation about the fate of our beloved planet. We cannot solve a problem we won't discuss. But now that the spell of silence has been broken, perhaps we can stay awake and go to work.

~~~~~~~~

I struggled to write this book. No one, including me, really wants to think about these overwhelming problems. In order to deal with the issues I wanted to write about, I had to come out of my own denial, connect dots I did not want to connect, face my own pain and sorrow, and finally accept reality. This process was one of the most painful of my life.

I also was reluctant to inflict suffering on readers. I want every one of you to be happy and have a positive experience when you are reading this book. With this topic it is a challenge to make that happen. I try to use humor and stories whenever I can. The most difficult material comes first. But it is soon finished. Then we will move into more heartening reading. Stay with me, please. Expect a turning.

If you are reading this book, you have already made a commitment to begin a voyage of discovery. Recognizing and naming problems is a huge step on this journey. Facing them emotionally demands courage and a certain trust in your own strength. I urge you to be gentle with yourself. You will traverse dark and stormy seas, but together we will come ashore at a new and hopeful place.

As a fellow traveler, I cannot hold myself up as a great success. I've failed many times to calm myself or to find a beacon on the shore—but I can reference myself as one who has made the trip. I know from experience that people can navigate this process and come out on the other side of the storm. While I don't pretend to be an expert guide for everyone, I hope to be a small lighthouse for you as you begin your own odyssey.

In its particulars your path will be different from mine and from everyone else's, but, at core, we are on the same journey. We are alive together in this moment on the green boat of Earth. We share the same desires to be respected, loved, and useful. And in spite of a possible impending calamity, we want and need to be able to relax and have fun. We are all entitled to the same basic human rights for a sustainable planet and a future for all living beings.

We humans are not without resources. We have our intelligence, humor, and compassion, our families and friends, and our ancestry of resilient hominid survivors. We can become the whole, authentic, and connected humans we were meant to be. Let's help each other with this.

TRAUMA

ONE

SOS

The Tidal Wave

*He who fights the future has
a dangerous enemy.*

SØREN KIERKEGAARD

Then

My first memory is a visual one, of dappled sunlight splashing through the green leaves of a tall tree. I was on a blanket in my grandmother's front yard in Sparta, Missouri. All I could see was sunshine playing peek-a-boo behind shimmering leaves and occasional explosions of white light when a sunbeam burst upon me unsheltered by the greenery. This first memory is also my first memory of beauty.

In the 1950s, my family lived in a small Nebraska town. When we drove down a highway at night, we could see in the headlights the white tails of jackrabbits hopping off the road. Tumbleweeds the size of armchairs blew across the car hood.

After a rain, the water in the ditches teemed with tadpoles and, at night, the music of frogs, which we called peepers, swelled in the background. Enormous prairie dog villages covered many fields. In the summer, our yard attracted bluebirds, magpies, bobolinks, and Baltimore orioles.

The seasons ebbed and flowed in predictable patterns, even though, of course, the day-by-day weather was often surprising. Crabapple and pear trees flowered in late March, peonies bloomed around Memorial Day, wheat was harvested the week of the Fourth of July, and shortly afterward we picked sweet corn. Wild plums were ripe in late September and our first snow often fell by the end of October or the beginning of November. On January first, New Year's Day, we played Monopoly and drank hot chocolate—it was too cold to go outside.

With the exception of those Nebraskans who lived in the sleepy cities of Lincoln and Omaha, almost all of us lived in little towns with sidewalks, alleys, open spaces, and cemeteries for the homesteaders. My town, Beaver City, was built around a square. I remember the old men in overalls who in good weather sat under the elm trees visiting with each other and teasing the children who walked by. Some of them chewed tobacco or sucked on a dreadful candy called horehound. Others gave us pennies or lollipops. We knew these men and their families and they knew us.

Most homes had front porches, but no air-conditioning. No one had televisions or home entertainment centers. After dinner in the evenings, when the weather permitted, people sat outside or walked around their neighborhoods chatting with their neighbors. We had a town whistle that told us when to eat breakfast, lunch, and dinner. At night, the sky was so clear I could lie on my front lawn and see the Milky Way, and sometimes even the northern lights.

We read the news once a week in our local newspaper or when *Time* magazine arrived. But most of the information that mattered to us was passed person to person more quickly than it could make it into print. We cared most about who had died, who was getting married, and who was born. We wanted to know who was buying a new car, when the baby chicks would arrive at the hatchery, who would play quarterback at the next football game, or if the high school band could afford new uniforms.

If we needed a pair of shorts or a sweater, our families ordered them by mail from Sears, Roebuck or J. C. Penney and waited several weeks for them to arrive. Men walked home from work for lunch and often took a nap before returning to their jobs. In the summer, children spent their days lolling around and swimming at the local pool. Stores closed at six at night and all day Sundays. Weekends were so slow that families often just drove around in the country or dropped in on friends for a visit.

One of my favorite memories is of the adults in my family asking me to go places with them. When they'd invite me to ride to the next town over or to a farm, they would often add, "I want you to keep me company."

In Beaver City, we were with the people we were with. Except for pen pals, letters, and expensive long-distance calls, we had no way of communicating with anyone else. I remember lying outside on a haystack with my friends at night and talking for hours about whatever floated to the surface of our consciousness.

This manageable universe lasted for me until October 1962, the year the USSR tried to ship missiles to Cuba. President Kennedy was concerned that the Soviets would use Cuba as a launching point to destroy the United States with nuclear weapons. He announced he would blockade Cuba to prevent the missiles from arriving near America's shores, a turn of events the press labeled the Cuban Missile Crisis.

I still remember that event. It was a strange, unsettling time. My father drove a hundred miles to pick me up from a Methodist Youth Fellowship retreat. I was playing jacks with my friends when my wild-eyed father rushed into the gym and hustled me out the door. In the car, he explained that because of what was happening in the world, we might have a nuclear attack, and he told me, "When all hell breaks loose, our family needs to be together."

He assured me that he had stored ample water, food, and blankets in our storm cellar. He said, "If we have to, we can last a month down there." As we drove home past the little Nebraska farms, we didn't speak again. We were both too frightened.

Luckily, the crisis simmered down. But it was then that I learned that faraway forces could destroy my world in a day and that my parents—that anyone's parents—really had no power to protect us children.

Now

Recently I was telling my grandchildren about all the things that didn't exist when I was a girl. I mentioned cell phones, the Internet, cruise control, blenders, microwaves, and television. The list was so long that my grandson asked, "Nonna, did they have apples when you were a girl?"

People are not the same today, either. They look and sound different. They carry more tension in their faces and bodies and more stress and exhaustion in their voices. Even children's faces look less innocent and more harried. And people behave differently, too. There's less joking, less singing in the shower, and fewer long, rambling conversations. People aren't as spontaneous. At grocery stores, concerts, or on the streets, when we meet people we care about and haven't seen for a long time we give them a few minutes of our time and then rush on to our important tasks.

People seem less focused and present. Often when I am talking to someone, I can tell the exact moment when they disappear from our conversation and "go to China," as Iowa songwriter Greg Brown would say.

So many aspects of life that I took for granted until quite recently seem to be deteriorating. As my friend Karen put it, "I can accept change, but nowadays all of the changes are for the worse."

I was curious how widespread this belief was, so I queried people about what kinds of positive cultural changes they'd witnessed. Some came up with a few examples, such as the rise of farmers' markets, an African American president, the restoration of the California condors, or emerging alternative energy sources. However, many people couldn't come up with a single positive change. Not one.

A colleague told me, "I feel as if everything is broken right now—in education, in health care, in the politics and the banking system." I noted that even the U.S. Postal Service, that Rock of Gibraltar of my youth, has been pounded into near bankruptcy because our government is unwilling to subsidize it.

On every level—international, national, and personal—the pace of change is such that it is hard for us to respond in adaptive and timely ways. As a school administrator told me, "Sometime in the early 1990s problems stopped being solvable." A friend put it this way: "There are no simple problems anymore."

My husband Jim and I can serve as examples of this confusion. We want to do the right thing, but it is increasingly hard to discern what the right thing is. Most problems, when carefully considered, seem to possess almost oceanic complexity. We are not sure what to eat, what products to buy, how best to travel, what charitable groups to support, and what authority figures to trust. We are skeptical of much "information." Jim and I have an old joke. Whenever I say that something or someone is driving me crazy, Jim responds, "That is not a drive, it's a short putt." That seems to apply to all of us now. We all feel a little too close to the edge.

People's increasing workload is called "speedup," which *Webster's* defines as "an employer's demand for accelerated output without increased pay." For example, hotel maids now clean three to four times as many rooms as they did fifteen years ago. In my town, Lincoln, the caseloads of human service workers have doubled or tripled. Schoolteachers not only have more students in their classrooms, but they have more students with serious learning and behavioral problems. Office workers often have so much work to do so quickly that they are hyperactive and disorganized.

We constantly are told—and we tell ourselves—that whatever topic is being considered is the most important thing. Every day we are admonished that it is essential to _____. We could fill in the blank in a thousand ways: develop our spiritual lives, eat organic fruits and vegetables, exercise regularly, stay connected to our extended family, research our options before we make a purchase, and make time for our friends. While all of these ideas are commendable, the sheer number of absolutely essential things we should do is ridiculous. Everything can't be the most important thing.

One of my neighbors, a single father, once took his three young children to the dentist. The dentist told him the kids weren't brushing their teeth properly and that he needed to do it for them for a week, spending about seven minutes twice a day teaching each child how to brush and floss properly. After that, the dentist suggested the dad observe them brush and floss for another week. When the neighbor told me he sighed and said, "How am I going to find forty minutes a day to watch my kids brush their teeth?"

This speedup pervades all aspects of life. Not only are people frenetic but, sadly, they don't have time to engage in those activities that would actually help them to alleviate their stress.

Via our machines—be it phone, television, or computer—

we receive an enormous amount of information every day. But we don't have the time, the energy, and the emotional resilience to deal with all of this information. We do triage as best we can, but we still are flooded with more stimulation than we can process and integrate.

Still, many people are hooked. Scientists have discovered that every time we hear the blip or ding of an e-mail or text message a small amount of dopamine is released into our brains. We humans are programmed to be curious and it is natural to want to know more, more, and more. Therapists have coined a phrase for a new addiction: FOMO, or "fear of missing out."

We cannot seem to dance fast enough. Most of us suffer from what Susan Moon calls "hurry sickness." During a visit to a meditation retreat in northern California, called Spirit Rock, I learned that even the most revered Tibetan Buddhist monks, who have spent their lives learning to be present and centered, have said that they're not certain they could stay calm if they lived in America.

Our bodies send us SOS signals via ailments such as high blood pressure, ulcers, headaches, and hives. At my last checkup, my dentist told me that something alarming was happening with her patients. For most of the years of her practice, the incidence of grinding teeth (called temporomandibular joint disorder, or TMJ) has been steady. However, in the last five years, she has noticed a meteoric increase in the percentage of patients with TMJ. She believes that this phenomenon can be explained only by the increasing stress in her patients' lives.

Trauma

Recently at dusk, on our way to Omaha for a concert, my husband Jim and I saw a wild tom turkey in the median of a busy highway. Somehow, crossing the road, the turkey had become trapped there with traffic buzzing by at fifty miles an hour and absolutely no way for him to cross to safety. We pulled off to the side of the road to strategize a rescue.

At first, the turkey was frantically running in circles. He appeared overheated and his beak was open. It seemed that he knew it was almost over for him. We discussed various rescue plans, but none seemed plausible. We felt sad and helpless. Finally, we couldn't bear to witness his suffering any longer. When someone else stopped and called Animal Rescue, we drove on.

We humans are much like that turkey. We are in a dangerous environment without much room to maneuver, and we are running out of time to fix things. Our fear, sorrow, and sense of hopelessness go far deeper than words. We want what we have always wanted and we make the same mistakes we have always made, but today the context is different. There are more of us; our destinies are more intertwined; and nothing less than the life cycle of our planet and the future of our species is at stake.

Trauma is the psychological experience of stress when our inner and outer resources are not sufficient to handle what we are facing. Certain conditions, such as war, dislocation from one's homeland, torture, rape, or the witnessing of grisly accidents or crimes, cause serious trauma in almost all people. But trauma also comes from being marooned in an airport while one's parent dies alone in a faraway hospital, from losing a job one desperately needs, and from lying awake at night worrying about an out-of-control teenager. Trauma can arise from knowing that the planet is dying and that we are not organizing ourselves to prevent that.

Most of us are suffering from mild to severe mid-traumatic stress disorder, a term coined by my friend Stephanie Sugars, who is engaged in a long-term battle with cancer. Usually trauma is discussed as post-traumatic stress disorder. We Americans are not post-trauma, but rather are engaged in an unfolding situation that is almost certain to worsen before it improves.

For some of us, trauma manifests as sorrow, and we find ourselves struggling every day to be happy and hopeful. For others, trauma sparks anger and irritability, and we find ourselves needing to apologize for our short tempers. Still others simply feel powerless and helpless.

I need not expound on our current stress and despair levels. You are experiencing it. Indeed, if you are paying attention to the world, you likely are in pain of some kind.

Mental health surveys show record numbers of people with depression and panic disorders. In 2012, the National Institute of Mental Health reported that 18 percent of adults suffer from anxiety disorders.

When life becomes unbearably painful, some people stop experiencing it. Over 10 percent of the U.S. population is taking antidepressants and one in eight has a problem with alcohol or street drugs. Remember the old joke, "I'd rather have a bottle in front of me than a frontal lobotomy." That is the solution many are embracing.

We have become a nation of ruminators and insomniacs. We feel frazzled and stressed and harried in ways we don't even understand. The fact that we cannot even grasp or acknowledge what is happening to ourselves makes it difficult not to feel isolated. If we are brave enough to face the truth and to share it with other people, often we are punished the way whistleblowers are always punished. That is, we are ostracized or considered troublemakers or overreactors.

By now, many of us have stopped believing in any kind of permanence. We don't assume the human race and other living species will persevere. We do not expect that the world's freshwater, coral reefs, air, fuel, or forests will last into our grandchildren's lifetimes. With the rise of gene-splicing, robotics, our rapidly evolving computer systems, and genetically modified everything, we do not even have a sense that humans will remain as the familiar organisms our grandmothers could describe. We have no faith that our futures will be better than our pasts.

Over the last decades, humans have sailed into an emotional hurricane that no one knows how to navigate. People still have their usual problems—we can't afford to fix the leaky roof or our child is failing social studies or our dog has fleas or our mother has Alzheimer's. But in addition to these, we are threatened by all kinds of global storms.

As a culture, we do not have constructive ways to think about and help each other think about how to handle the Great Acceleration and our global storms. Our burdens themselves are strange because even though they have to do with the entire human history of technology and the whole world in all its complexity, at the same time, they are personal issues. After all, each one of us wakes up in the morning, faces a daunting day, somehow propels through it, and falls in bed exhausted at night, our to-do list not completed and our needs for relaxation, companionship, laughter, and leisure often unmet. What is happening to us?

The Great Acceleration of Human Impact on the Planet

The trauma of our personal lives and the rapidity of the deterioration of our planet are deeply connected. Hominids have been around for at least two million years and homo sapiens for two hundred thousand. Yet it is only in the last 250 years that as a species we have changed the core systems of the planet. The atmospheric scientist Paul Crutzen calls this span of time the Anthropocene. Humans are changing our earth's biological and chemical composition. Unless we make radical changes, the Anthropocene will be painfully and sadly short.

We now face problems that we can barely name and that we do not understand. As we struggle to cope with the daily tempests and the continuous tidal wave of troubling information, such as the slaughter of the Syrians by their government or the information that half the coral reefs are at risk, we feel many emotions at once. We experience our own grief, but also the pain of the earth and of people suffering all over the world.

Writers are inventing terms to try to describe this new set of emotions. Environmentalist Joanna Macy calls this pain "planetary anguish." Daniel Goleman coined "eco-angst." And Glenn Albrecht created "solastalgia" to describe "a type of homesickness or melancholia that you feel when you are at home and your home environment is changing all around you in ways that you feel are profoundly negative."

Even people who enjoy lives filled with friends, family, and good work know that our world is simultaneously falling apart. We sense it when we cross bridges with no rivers below or look out on miles of tract homes in what only a few years earlier had been wheat fields or meadows. We are heartbroken when we see pictures of the oily pelican or the stranded polar bear.

Yet we naturally resist upsetting information about the state of our planet, with its implied responsibility for doing something to help save it. Terry Tempest Williams wrote about the Gulf Coast after Hurricane Katrina in *Orion* magazine. She told truths far scarier and more devastating than many of the details reported by mainstream media. Yet, after she wrote it, she reflected, "Who do I send this to? Who really wants to read this sad news?"

Sociologist Barbara Katz Rothman has a phrase for information that makes life seem ever more complicated and disturbing than it already is. She calls it "incapacitating knowledge." When we are on overload, almost all information can become incapacitating knowledge. Lately I've been using the term "distractionable intelligence" in contrast to "actionable intelligence." Distractionable intelligence gives us no ideas for action but upsets us greatly.

One night before dinner Jim asked me to sit and have a

glass of wine with him. That day he had overseen the installation of a new heating and air-conditioning system after a tree had crushed our old one. That same week our refrigerator needed to be replaced. And suddenly our dishwasher wasn't working properly, either. I'd been writing and working hard at the time and I said, "I'll sit down with you as long as we don't have to discuss the fate of the earth." Jim agreed readily and added, "I don't even want to discuss the fate of our appliances."

An example of the crushing power of good information without actionable intelligence comes from a night when Jim and I attended a lecture by a Nobel Prize–winning scientist on the topic of the climate crisis. We had to push ourselves to go. It was a rainy night and both of us wanted to read by the fire. However, we decided it was important to support speakers like this. So we found ourselves sitting in a large, windowless university classroom beside students who were required to attend and their professors.

The scholar knew his science. He gave a PowerPoint presentation with graph after dismal graph, lines running up at alarming slopes to alarming heights. He convinced the already-convinced that the brink of doom was nigh. But his presentation was humorless, dull, and utterly devoid of hope.

Equally important, the scientist didn't speak to the most crucial questions. What do we do about this? What are the effective ways to make changes in ourselves, in our communities, and in our policies?

To be fair, the speaker was a climate scientist, not an expert on changing behavior. Yet, after he delivered his terrifying information, he suggested we ride our bikes, use energy-saving bulbs, and recycle. Any middle school student could have made those recommendations.

By the end, I was almost too whipped to walk out of the classroom. While I respected the man's knowledge and his effort to educate the public about our situation, I felt as if I never wanted to attend another lecture on global climate change.

I felt dispirited that I'd wasted a perfectly good evening. I wasn't upset about the information. I knew it already. But I was despondent about the lack of help and hope in the speaker's message. I better understood all the people I'd encountered who didn't want to hear lectures on environmental collapse. I thought to myself that if this is the message and this man the messenger, then we are in even deeper trouble than I thought.

I was sure that this lecture would not lead to uplift and action. I could see the resignation in the faces in the audience. Of course we need good, solid information. But equally critical is how and when information is delivered.

Psychologists know that delivering too much bad news at once leads to emotional shutdown. But sugarcoating facts doesn't inspire positive change, either. In therapy, clients need a certain amount of anxiety to propel them toward change, but not so much as to discourage their hopeful efforts. Therapy should be tailored to each client. This mix of optimism and anxiety is difficult to get right one person at a time and is almost impossible when talking to or writing for large groups of people.

How do we extrapolate from the therapy session to the culture? How do we change a country's thinking and behavior about global climate change and other overwhelming issues?

Climate educators must balance information with action suggestions, motivational elements, and aspirational framing. If we want people to listen to and process traumatic information, then we must be able to frame that information in ways that allow our listeners to be hopeful and calm.

Information must be carefully paired with people's emotional ability to absorb and process it. We must not only be able to acknowledge and talk about a problem, but we must also be able to conceptualize it in ways that allow people to act upon it as human beings.

DENIAL

TWO

Even God Can't Sink This Ship

Shock and Disbelief

*All truth goes through three steps. First, it
is ridiculed, then it is violently opposed, and
finally it is accepted as self-evident.*

ARTHUR SCHOPENHAUER

*It takes two to speak the truth—
one to speak it and the other to hear it.*

HENRY DAVID THOREAU

The first hominids emerged from Africa and spread out
across Europe and Asia. What we know from anthropology reveals that we have always been an unpredictable species, capable of both empathy and violence, enterprise and
self-destruction.

Humans may be the one species capable of denial. We can
believe more than one thing at once, and we can hold beliefs

about our beliefs. We can lie to ourselves and even convince ourselves that what we are saying is true. Our common human ability to delude ourselves, while no doubt useful in certain circumstances, has caused us a great deal of trouble and suffering over the millennia.

Our capacity for self-delusion has been evident since the beginning of recorded history, but at no time perhaps more than in the present moment. Currently, we are proceeding as if—in spite of all evidence—things are certain to work out in the end. In fact, the human race is not too big to fail.

In *States of Denial: Knowing About Atrocities and Suffering*, Stanley Cohen examines the individual and societal ways of denying reality that can lead to atrocities like the Holocaust. He asks, "How could so many smart people know the situation and do nothing?" He finds that ordinary Germans could not tolerate knowing that terrible things were happening to their neighbors and friends and knowing, at the same time, that they were not acting in ways to protect them. Holding this much dissonance made people crazy. In order to defend themselves psychologically, people denied and minimized the atrocities and exaggerated their own helplessness. After the war, many people within sight of the crematoriums said, "I didn't see anything." Or, "What could we do? We'd be killed if we said anything." And while it is true that it was dangerous to be helpful, people could have done more in many cases than they actually did.

Cohen defines denial as simply "the need to be innocent of a troubling recognition." He notes that denial is a "willful ignorance," a knowledge that is not being faced. When we are in denial, we both know and don't know what is going on.

Groups have always had the capacity for persistent self-delusion. During World War I, men were ordered to march toward each other, guns firing, which led to the slaughter en masse of hundreds of thousands of young soldiers. The Battle of the Somme, which lasted from July through November 1916, resulted in over a million casualties. At the end of this battle, the British and French had almost nothing to show for their bloody offensive.

Why didn't the generals realize their stupid and destructive strategies and reconsider their plans? We will never know, but I suspect cognitive dissonance was involved. They couldn't bear the emotional pain of knowing that their blunders had resulted in the deaths of hundreds of thousands of good men.

In the documentary *The Fog of War*, former defense secretary Robert McNamara talked about how, as the failures in the Vietnam War increased, the clarity of thinking decreased. He called this fuzzy, imprecise way of evaluating the situation the "fog of war."

Watching the movie *Gasland*, about the impact of natural gas fracking on land and water, I found myself thinking about McNamara's words. *Gasland* demonstrates that all the water in our country flows together and that we are allowing corporations to poison it. But our country has yet to have a serious conversation about protecting our water. We are not in a "fog of war" as much as we are in a "fog of climate collapse."

The Nature of Our Problem

Humans are not responding adaptively to the compelling information on our global storm because of the particular nature of the problems. We are better at solving concrete rather than abstract problems and immediate rather than distant ones. Most people in industrialized nations deal reasonably well with car accidents and house fires. We've seen them, at least on television, and we understand the importance of preparedness and safety regulations. But nobody on the planet has experienced the totality of our impending global catastrophe.

Our responses to threats are strongest when they have immediate personal impacts and a direct cause. Humans like quick fixes and certainty of results. We like to solve the problem and move on. Our global storm is invisible, unprecedented, drawn out, and caused by us all. For most people, at least so far, it has only indirect personal impacts.

For a variety of reasons, global climate change is not intuitively obvious. The weather has always been changeable. For a while scientists called the wildly unstable weather "global warming," which led to puzzled questions such as "How can it be global warming if it's cooler this winter?" Even now, after overwhelming scientific consensus on climate change, we are still discussing the issue as if it were a belief, not a fact. This skepticism and debate hampers our ability to respond adaptively to our situation. Not surprisingly, we do better at solving problems when we all agree they exist.

Think of Pearl Harbor. Before the bombing of American

bases in Honolulu in 1941, Americans were aware and uneasy about the world situation. They believed in the possibility of war with Germany and Japan, but there was no consensus about what America's response should be. After the bombing, President Roosevelt was said to be relieved to finally have a direct emergency to deal with rather than a creeping catastrophe. Secretary of Labor Frances Perkins said, "I think the boss must have a great load off his mind. . . . At least we know what to do now." It was a sense of knowing what our cultural responses should be that was so liberating and empowering.

With World War II, there was a known enemy and an immediate shared sense of mission. Our climate crisis presents us with the opposite scenario. It is difficult to convince humans to act when the payoffs are uncertain while the sacrifices are substantial and immediate. Try telling a young couple to skip cable TV because they may need that money for retirement. Or attempt to convince a hungry teenager to pass up a chance to buy pizza and instead save his money for college.

Our resistance to accepting global climate change and its implications reminds me of my chain-smoking, emphysemic client named Sally. Several years ago Sally hauled her oxygen tank and a pack of cigarettes into my office. Her doctor had told her that unless she quit smoking she had only a few months to live.

Of course Sally knew all the scientific information about the health hazards of smoking. Everyone who loved her had begged her to stop. Yet, for decades, Sally had resisted change. Over time she had developed a legion of defenses with which to fight reality, the primary one being "I'll quit tomorrow."

Sally also had to contend with an issue that often makes

behavioral change a battle. While the cumulative effects of smoking several packs a day over the next few months would most certainly kill her, any one cigarette would not make much difference. And, while dying from cigarettes in the future was an abstract concept, smoking a cigarette right now made her feel better. Long term, she agreed she needed to stop. But she could quit next week or after her birthday. Yet, in spite of all the resistance and the obstacles, Sally knew her current lifestyle was not sustainable. A part of her wanted to change, if only she could believe it possible.

Facing and coping with our global storm presents the same dilemmas Sally faced. We humans must struggle with our preferences for definite short-term pleasures versus possible long-term gains. Especially in traumatic situations, most of us think short term and seek immediately soothing comforts.

We also must wrestle with a problem of scale. The human mind is designed to cope with a different magnitude of threats. Humans have spent 95 percent of our history as hunter-gatherers and we are still hardwired for this life. We are built to find food and shelter, reproduce, spot nearby dangers, and enjoy being with others. It's almost impossible for us to grasp problems on a global scale with our Neolithic brains. It's like trying to picture 200 million pinto beans.

Years ago I observed that the U.S. Senate passed a billion-dollar bill for NASA with almost no debate. Then the senators wrangled for hours about small policies related to coffee breaks, the cafeteria, and parking fees. I thought to myself, "They don't really know what NASA is doing. But everyone has a point of view about how often he needs a coffee break and how much coffee and parking should cost."

Almost all of us are capable of feeling sad if our favorite park gets destroyed or our water source becomes contaminated. Many of us would climb a tree to rescue a cat. But we find it much harder to respond emotionally to the deforestation of the Amazon or the pollution of a faraway ocean. We simply don't have the emotional bandwidth necessary to address global problems.

Finally, the human race is more likely to solve a problem that requires a hammer if we have the hammer at hand. We can soothe a crying baby or notify the police when we see our neighbor's windows are broken. We can put a bucket under a leaky ceiling or find a blanket on a chilly night. We have the tools to fix those problems. For global environmental problems, we don't have a hammer.

Even God Can't Sink This Ship

We humans are programmed to respond to threats by fleeing or fighting. Our global storm will not let us do either. Our problems feel too big to fight and there is no place we can flee to, so we feel paralyzed. We are in a crisis that is too scary to confront and too important to ignore. "Willful ignorance" occurs when it feels wrong to acknowledge and wrong not to acknowledge a situation. This leads to crazy-making attempts to balance precariously between awareness and denial.

I noticed this balancing act when on January 30, 2012, it was seventy degrees in Nebraska. Weather is not climate, but extreme weather over a large area for a long period of time can be a climate signal. The high temperatures in winter 2012 all over the United States may well have been a climate signal.

That January, when I ran into people in the stores and on the streets, they remarked about the lovely spring weather, but then they'd seem a little confused by their attitude. A few mumbled something such as "This doesn't feel right" or "This didn't happen when I was young." Many people appeared to know and not know that our weather was affected by something other than chance variation. But they didn't know how to acknowledge this. They were afraid of the pain of speaking in a straightforward way. As my husband said, "If we were not speaking in code, we would be holding each other and crying."

Another problem we face is that apocalyptic language has been around for thousands of years and many of us are numb to it. A graduate student told me recently, "I am twenty-five years old and I have been told the world was about to end since I was in kindergarten. I just don't pay attention anymore." One of my friends said, "I thought I would die during the nuclear scares of the sixties. We practiced Duck and Cover at elementary school. I wasted time being upset about what I couldn't control." She shook her head and smiled sadly. "I won't go to dark places in my mind anymore. I am careful to divert myself with mysteries and cooking shows." I understand my friends' points of view. We all have experienced a lot of crying wolf about the apocalypse. But our problem this time is different—the wolf is at the door.

Our desire to avoid confronting ecological issues is understandable. We want to be happy and optimistic. We want to relax and have fun. We want to think we live in a stable universe and that the human race has a future. And, like all humans since the beginning of time, we want to feel calm, safe, and protected. We yearn to feel a sense of agency and control. All of these legitimate needs keep us from confronting our environmental problems. Besides, most of us feel as if we have enough on our plates without taking on the deterioration of the biosphere.

In this sense, my friend Deb is typical. She works eighty hours a week at the Center for People in Need, an organization that helps the unemployed, the disabled, and the refugee populations. She recently lost her husband and her stepfather. Thinking about the pending environmental catastrophe makes her sad and she already has enough sorrow on her plate. She doesn't believe she has much power to help and she is already overwhelmed by her demanding job, her ill mother, and her own health problems.

She believes in human-made climate change, but she only thinks about it when she hears stories of extreme weather events. Then she finds herself asking, "Why isn't someone doing more about this?" She feels guilty that she doesn't recycle, but she says she is too old to change. Still, Deb is trying to help her grandchildren appreciate the earth. She likes to take them to parks and on picnics. When she and the grandchildren discussed a book they had read together about endangered polar bears, she told them, "That is because humans are not caring for the earth."

The last time we talked, though, Deb told me about a conversation she'd had with her nine-year-old granddaughter. Renae said, "I know a secret, something you don't know." Then Renae told Deb about global climate change and Deb admitted she knew about it, too.

Renae was shocked and asked, "How did you find out?"

Deb responded, "I read it in the papers and I heard about it on the nightly news. How do you know about it?"

"We learned in school." Renae sighed and added, "I thought I knew something you didn't." Then she asked, "Grandma, why don't we ever talk about this?"

Deb said that she would like to talk about it.

Renae responded, "Then I could teach you more about it. I could teach you to recycle."

Deb agreed and said, "That is how I'll learn."

It's noteworthy that what influenced Deb was love, not fear. She rethought her position when confronted with a beloved messenger, one who, we can hope, has a long future ahead of her.

We humans cannot blame ourselves for resisting traumatic information. Our minds are complex ecosystems. Procrastination, avoidance, and confusion are part of our nature. Research in two fields of psychology—selective attention and confirmation bias—shows that values and preconceived ideas determine receptivity to facts.

Selective attention is our tendency to orient toward only part of the environment at hand and to ignore other equally obvious parts. Confirmation bias is our inclination to seek evidence that confirms our existing beliefs. Beliefs can make people impervious to evidence and, in fact, lead to a scornful attitude toward science and its primary principles of investigation.

Psychological studies in what's called "inattentional blindness" help us understand another reason we have trouble grasping our situation. These studies teach us that when people are distracted and pay attention to many things at once, they often fail to notice something that is plainly visible. The best known of these studies is the Invisible Gorilla Test, conducted by Daniel Simons and Christopher Chabris. In this study, subjects watched a short video in which two groups of people (wearing black and white T-shirts) passed a basketball around. The subjects were told either to count the number of passes made by one of the teams or to keep count of bounce passes versus aerial passes.

While the game was going on, a woman walked through the scene wearing a full gorilla suit. After watching the video, the subjects were asked if they had seen anything out of the ordinary. Over 50 percent of the research subjects did not notice the gorilla. These results indicate that focusing intently on one detail significantly affects our ability to perceive other events.

These studies demonstrate how complicated the concept of denial is. It involves perception, attention, and memory, as well as values. If denial is not carried to extremes, it helps us to stay calm, focused, and positive. We have a healthy tendency to avoid thinking much about what we cannot control. Take death, for example. At some level, we all know that, ultimately, one way or another, we will say good-bye to everyone we love. However, for good reasons, we don't think about this every waking moment.

Sometimes we need to take a break from thinking about possible catastrophes. When Karen and I discussed the BP oil spill one day, she said, "I need to stop talking about this. My head is starting to hurt." I know how she feels. We want to savor a shrimp cocktail without, say, thinking about the loss of mangrove forests in East Asia. We want to be able to drive to our child's ball games without worrying about carbon units. We all need time to replenish ourselves and appreciate the miracle of life.

Most of us are good at "forgetting" our planet's dire situation. Often this kind of forgetting signals that we are at a place of great pain and anxiety, that something terrible has just happened or is happening and we are striving to keep it from awareness. It is as if certain topics are crime scenes with yellow tape all around them saying, "Do Not Enter."

Kathryn Rheem calls attention to what is not being said "attuning to avoidance." As a therapist, I learned to tune in to my clients' "disconnects." I watched for the unspoken conversations manifested by disconnects between words and body language or facial expressions, between the content and the emotions of a message, or between expressed feelings and behavior.

For example, a teenage bully was referred to me by his school for counseling. He arrived with his father, who narrated events as if his son were indeed a troubled and mean youth. However, the father laughed when he described his son's cruel behavior. His tone showed a disconnect between his son's actions and his own emotional response to them.

With environmental issues, these disconnects are rampant. There is an enormous gap between what scientists know and what most people know. And there is a gap between what is actually happening and what we perceive. Furthermore, even if we know the facts, there are gaps between what we know and what we say and what we think and what we do. As one of my friends lamented recently, "I know what is going on and yet, oh, my God, I am still using a clothes dryer."

All of us can find these disparities in ourselves. In theory, we all could be doing ten thousand things to make a difference. The list could include everything from buying green cleaning supplies to running for public office on a sustainability platform. It could include riding a bike to work, buying an electric car, using a worm bin for composting, and raising our own chickens in the backyard or on our apartment building's rooftop. Logic shows us that we will do only a small percentage of the things we potentially could do. We have other concerns and only twenty-four hours in a day.

As we recognize our own disconnects, we can begin to make more intentional decisions with the many small choices we have every day. But in order to do that, we must first understand the complexities of our own systems of denial.

The Ways Humans Defend Themselves from Too Much Reality

1. They deny reality entirely.

Some people don't really keep up with any news of the day so they genuinely are unaware of what is happening. "Is global climate change the name of a rock band?" this kind of person might ask. However, most deniers are actively defending themselves against information that would make them uneasy.

As a general rule, I don't talk long to climate change deniers. From sad experience I have learned that it is impossible to change their minds. A few years ago I had a conversation with my neighbor Max, an inveterate climate change denier. I lent him some articles and talked about scientific evidence. After one agonizingly long and fruitless discussion, Max said, "You can believe whatever you want and so can I. I don't care about your evidence. I just know it isn't happening."

This reminds me of an old therapist in-joke about reasoning with a schizophrenic. A man on the psychotic unit at a mental health hospital believed he was dead. Thinking to trick him with logic, the young therapist asked, "Do you think dead men bleed?" The man who was schizophrenic answered, "Of course not." Then the therapist pricked his finger and made it bleed slightly. He asked the man, "What do you think of that?" The man with schizophrenia replied, "Well, I guess dead men bleed."

Scientists have worked to educate Americans about our climate chaos, but on a cultural level, nothing has been working, or at least nothing is working fast enough to save us. In almost any form it is delivered, people have resisted environmental information for years. Despite evidence stretching back for decades, including the formation of the Intergovernmental Panel on Climate Change (IPCC) in 1988, many people remain uninformed. A report by the Yale Project on Climate Change Communication and the George Mason University Center for Climate Change Communication, called

"Global Warming's Six Americas in May 2011," found that 25 percent of Americans are dismissive and doubtful about the reality of global climate change.

2. They accept some aspect of reality but deny other equally critical aspects.

In an airport, a man noticed that I was reading *Hot: Living Through the Next Fifty Years on Earth*. He leaned toward me and said conspiratorially, "You know that is alarmist bullshit."

I asked him, "Do you think the world's weather is changing?"

He replied, "The changes are just part of a natural cycle. CO_2 doesn't heat up the atmosphere. The sun heats the earth."

I asked him what he thought would happen in the next centuries and he replied, "I think the sun will cool back down and everything will work out fine in the end."

I said I respectfully disagreed with him and quickly walked off to buy a sandwich.

3. They minimize or normalize.

Over the years, I've heard many people respond to our global storm by saying, "There have always been doomsayers." Or, "It is not as bad as they say." Back when the phrase for what was happening was "global warming," I heard many people respond by just joking, "I can do without winter." Or, "I'll build a swimming pool." Following these comments, the speaker usually poured a stiff drink or lit up a cigarette.

4. They overemphasize our lack of power.

I have heard people say things such as "The human race is toast. Soon the only living animals will be cockroaches." The twin of this helpless kind of thinking is to overestimate the possibilities of rescue by technology, UFOs, celebrities, or God. These convenient illusions preclude any true efforts to rethink our situation and change our behavior.

The idea that we are powerless quickly becomes a self-fulfilling prophecy. If we don't think we can change anything, why even try? In fact, we create our power with our actions. When we decide we want to have influence, we can find ways to make that happen. These past few years have been filled with examples of ordinary people deciding to exert their power and doing so effectively. *Time* dubbed 2011 "the Year of the Protester." Its cover photo was of a protester. All over the world, from Tunis to Tampico, we saw sparkling examples of people who refused to believe they were powerless and set about to see what they could accomplish.

5. They deny their emotional investment in reality.

I have heard grandparents shrug off the issue by saying, "It's not my problem. I won't be around when it happens." They then laugh weakly. I don't laugh. I know my friends well enough to know that they simply can't bear to think of their grandchildren suffering. That thought is so terrible to them that they don't allow it in.

Some people are fatalistic. As my doctor once put it, "It's just as well. Man is a cancer. The earth will be better off without us." Of course, my doctor works hard to keep me alive. And I am sure he doesn't think the world is better off without his own children and grandchildren.

I recently had lunch with a librarian. I asked her what she felt when she thought about global climate change. She paused, then said carefully, "It's a midlevel worry." She mentioned a book called *The World Without Us*. She said, "The planet might be better off without humans. I comfort myself with that thought." I thought to myself, which humans? Is the planet better off without Rumi, Shakespeare, Mozart, Ai Weiwei, or Wangari Maathai?

6. They compartmentalize.

People deliberately disconnect the dots between knowledge, emotional responses, and behavior. Many people believe the science and know the timelines, but they do not act on the implications. For example, grandparents often save money for the children in the family. They hope that in twenty years their sacrifice will mean a college fund, a down payment on a first house, or a financial cushion for emergencies. Saving for the distant future was a sensible idea forty years ago and I still do it myself. It feels right. But given the enormity of our global problems, these actions seem almost quaint. Realistically, our children and grandchildren are more likely to live long and happy lives if we work tirelessly to save the earth's resources today.

Of course we want our children to be happy and safe in the future. But, as the evidence shows, twenty years from now, they may not have breathable air or potable water, let alone jobs, colleges, and suburban homes. Even the world's richest man cannot buy a new ozone layer for his grandkids.

7. They feign apathy.

Many people simply say they are not interested in the topic. However, what looks like apathy or indifference is often pain and confusion. Renee Lertzman published a study called "The Myth of Apathy." She interviewed people about global climate change and found that people actually care intensely about the environment, but that their emotions are tangled up and upsetting and they are so beset by internal conflicts that they cannot act adaptively. They are not apathetic, but rather in psychological shutdown. A metaphor for this "apathy" could be white light, which looks like one color or even the absence of color, but really is all of the colors combined, somehow canceling each other out.

8. They kill the messenger.

Climate change deniers often demonize the scientists and environmentalists who try to warn and protect them. They label activists as extremists. Often people confuse engagement in participatory democracy with being a radical. When we share mainstream and commonsense goals such as clean water, preserving our oceans and forests, or stopping fossil fuel industries from destroying our beautiful country, we are not radicals. We are just ordinary citizens willing to make sacrifices to save our world. We are no more extremists than are firefighters who are willing to sacrifice their lives to rescue people and animals.

~~~~~~~~

I suspect there are many more ways that Americans defend themselves against upsetting information about our global storm, but this list is a sampling. We are creative in our defenses. If you recognize yourself and everyone you know on this list, don't feel bad. We are all on the list. Welcome to our club!

Whatever categories we fall into, we all struggle with how to respond appropriately and still be happy. To stay present with the truth and its implications would feel like keeping our hand on a hot stove all the time. In real life almost all of us land in a category that could be called "riddled with contradictions."

Our emotional and physical survival depends on our ability to tolerate reality at least some of the time. We cannot act adaptively if we don't face the hard truths of the day. Most forms of denial don't lead to adaptive coping strategies. Emotions exist because they are evolutionarily adaptive. All emotions, even negative ones, are here to teach us something. We ignore them at great peril.

Our defenses are never completely successful. We cannot drown our sorrows, because it turns out they can swim. Anxiety seeps through. All of our energy goes into denial. We experience an emotional deadness. Our minds tangle with themselves. Instead we feel anger, lethargy, anxiety, and emptiness. We lose our vitality, joy, and sense of wonder. Most important, we lose our power to act in meaningful ways to create the world we want to see.

Joel Sartore is a man well experienced in the effects of human denial. He is a *National Geographic* photographer who lives in Lincoln, Nebraska, but he has traveled all over the world to photograph endangered species. Currently he is working on the Biodiversity Project. Half of the world's plants and animals are threatened with extinction in the near future. Joel wants to take their photos to show people what is at stake and to motivate them to act while they still can. He has taken pictures of over 1,800 species so far.

On the topic of the environment, he can be a heartbroken man. Joel told me that once a year all the *National Geographic* photographers meet. "After a year of work all over the world, we tell each other one horror story after another." He said, "We share our trauma and grief stories about what we have seen and give each other therapy." Joel has photographed Africa for years, and now when he flies over the big parks, he sees the roads and pipelines that are being built. He told me, "Soon all the lions, big mammals, and mountain gorillas will be extinct."

When we last had coffee together, Joel was dour. "Human overpopulation is the runaway train that will kill us all. In many parts of the world there are too many people for the land to carry." He cited Uganda as an example. It has thirty-two million citizens and its land can sustain only eight million people.

Joel has been following species extinctions since he was nine years old. At that time Joel was reading a *Look* magazine and saw a picture of Martha, the last passenger pigeon, who had expired many years earlier, on September 1, 1914. The article explained that these birds could fly sixty miles an hour and were so numerous that they could block out the sun in a given locale for three days at a time. That article gave Joel his first sense of how finite a species could be. He decided he wanted to do something that encouraged people to save animals. A few years later, he realized his photographs could do that.

As an adult, Joel spends his time alerting the world about species that are on the brink of extinction. He has photographed the last survivors of three different species of frog in the Amazon Basin. These frogs are disappearing because of habitat loss and changing rainfall patterns. For their eggs to hatch, they must be in cool, moist, fog-shrouded places.

I'd seen these frog pictures and also his photos of the Columbia Basin pygmy rabbit and of the last member of a salmon species on the Snake River. I told him, "I remember these photos because they made me cry."

Changing his focus to another part of the world, he said, "In parts of the Arctic, the Inuit tell me that the ice fades much earlier and comes back later. They are seeing slush for the first time." He told me, "If you were to hear what I have heard about overfishing, you would never eat fish again."

Joel believes that Americans don't remember even the last few decades well enough to realize what we are losing. He told me a story from a tour guide in California. The guide said, "Twenty years ago, when I took tourists out, we saw around three hundred blue sharks a day. The tourists loved it and were excited. Ten years ago, we saw ten a day and my customers loved that, too. Now it can take three days to spot a blue shark, but people still come out and are thrilled if they see one."

"Americans really don't like to hear bad news," Joel said. "I try to be entertaining when I talk about serious issues, but it doesn't always work." He told me about a speech he'd made for the National Geographic Society. He showed slides, talked about what was happening around the globe, and told stories and jokes. He said, "The crowd laughed and cried during my speech and I received a standing ovation. However, one woman wrote the event organizer to say she resented hearing sad news. She wrote, 'I just wanted to be entertained.'"

When he meets resistance and denial, he says to his audience, "I urge you to keep an open mind. Only a fool never changes his mind. I am telling you what I have seen. Draw your own conclusions."

Joel has his discouraging days. Once in Aspen he spoke at what was billed as a climate conference but what was, in fact, an example of cultural miseducation. After his own talk, Joel listened to four speakers in a row stand up and deny the existence of global climate change.

He made a face at me and said, "I couldn't believe it." He continued, "Right out the window behind them was a mountain covered with dead pine trees. This death of the great forests of the Rockies is happening because a pine beetle that used to die off every winter can now survive our warmer winters and spread."

That day, Joel was in despair. But most of the time, he fends off his sorrow and anger with his work. He has made it his mission to educate Americans about species loss and environmental collapse. And unlike the scientist I mentioned in the last chapter, Joel does this in a skillful and fascinating way. His photography and other efforts to communicate about our global situation are an example of a transcendent response.

Loving the world as Joel does almost always creates an intense combination of anguish and amazement. In particular, in America—because of our history, politics, media, and culture—it is easy to despair. But since America is one of the most stunningly beautiful, resource-rich places on earth, it's also easy to be amazed.

THREE

Our Foundering Ship of State

America, America

Do you think we can keep doing
this without paying a price?

BARBARA KINGSOLVER

The great advantage of the Americans
consists in their being able to commit faults
which they may afterwards repair.

ALEXIS DE TOCQUEVILLE

In his book *Collapse*, Jared Diamond examines the history of cultures that faced ecological catastrophes and the choices they made in their crucible moments. Some cultures, mired in denial and shock, were unable to save themselves from extinction. On Easter Island, residents cut down every single tree in order to build large statues in the sands, and then they all died of starvation. In Norse Greenland, people starved to death because they wouldn't plant crops or raise livestock that could survive in the area. They also refused to eat salmon in a place crisscrossed by salmon streams.

Other cultures developed new and more sustainable customs around population control, diet, and land use. They were able to face reality, deal with it adaptively, and continue to thrive. People in Iceland and New Guinea changed farming and eating habits as the climate changed. Diamond found that the primary difference between failed and surviving cultures was their willingness to acknowledge their situation and plan accordingly. Reading Diamond's book, I could not help but think that America's fossil-fuel-dependent civilization is on its way to his "failed" category. We may still have the potential to save ourselves, but we need to emerge quickly from our trance and get to work.

As a nation, we have yet to come to grips with our situation. The complex and multifaceted nature of our global storm somehow seems to push our culture into confusion and overload. Our energy policies, our fuel emission standards, our lack of care for our most vital resources—food, water, air, and soil—and our lack of emphasis on conservation and efficiency, all speak to the fact that our ship is foundering under the burden of these unarticulated problems. And we are barely even moving the deck chairs.

In 1988, James Hansen of NASA told the Senate that global warming had begun. Almost twenty-five years later, our American culture has yet to assimilate this information into our worldview. Our media outlets pay attention to the rise and fall of the Dow Jones Industrial Average, but not to species extinction rates. In this country money is well organized, but survival is not.

Six million people have seen *An Inconvenient Truth* and yet most Americans do not think much about ecological problems. A 2010 Pew Research poll asked Americans to rank twenty-one major problems in order of importance. By default, climate change ranked twenty-first on the list. The researchers said it wouldn't even have been twenty-first if the participants had had any other choices to put ahead of it. Pew Research polls taken in September 2011 revealed that, in spite of increasing evidence, belief in climate change was at its lowest level since 1997. In fact, it had decreased from 71 percent to 57 percent in the previous eighteen months.

By April 13, 2012, after fifteen thousand temperature records were broken across the country in March, attitudes were changing slightly. A Yale poll conducted around the same time showed that seven in ten Americans now believed that global warming was affecting the weather. Thirty-five percent of Americans believed they were affected by climate-change-related weather disasters in the previous year.

Even the manner in which Americans discuss global climate change is odd. We don't talk about "believing in" the laws of aerodynamics, the DNA code, or bacteria. By now the evidence for climate change is solid and the scientific community is united. Why do we speak of believing in it as if we were speaking of belief in extraterrestrials or ghosts?

All cultures have rules about what can and can't be acknowledged. In a *Yes!* magazine article, George Marshall discusses what sociologist Kari Norgaard calls the "cultural blocking of information." There are norms of attention and ways of selectively framing certain topics that keep them "out of range." An example of this in American discourse is either/or framing. For example, "Either you don't drive a car or you had better be quiet about the fossil fuel industry's greediness and environmental record." In fact, we could also talk about fuel-efficient cars, Zipcars, and cars that run on renewable energy. We could discuss incentives to drive less or carpool.

Norgaard believes that our denial of global warming is the result of social taboos. She finds that most people are deeply distressed about climate change, but they manage their guilt and anxiety by avoiding the topic. In America it is almost as if relevant information about our climate crisis is classified. Our national policy toward the devastation we face is, "Don't ask. Don't tell."

To experience what Norgaard is talking about, think about the reactions you would generate if you introduced the topic of our global storm at a social gathering. If you are like me that thought makes you uncomfortable. We prefer to be relaxed and attuned to the people around us. We don't want to appear gloomy, weird, or depressed. We don't like to criticize our government or business community. Most of us hate to start arguments and we worry that we will be viewed as proselytizers.

It is painful to discuss environmental issues with others because, when we try, we crash into their self-protective mechanisms, such as guilt and defensiveness. As the situation becomes more serious, we can expect to see more denial in our citizens. That is, we will if we don't change our norms of attention and talk to each other honestly.

Many citizens are more worried about global climate change than our politicians appear to be. When people talk openly to each other, they often voice concern and even alarm. Recently, I was in a garden store buying tarp to cover a weedy area. The young clerk mentioned the tarp would be more effective if I bought weed killer. I told him that I didn't believe in using weed killer. He was quiet as he rang me up, then he whispered to me that he didn't believe in using this toxic chemical, either.

That same week, when I went to the university for a swim, the young guy who checked me in was reading *Ishmael* by Daniel Quinn. When I told him how much I had enjoyed that book, he started to cry. He said the book had totally changed his life and he now wanted a different kind of world. I was struck by the sincerity of these young men, but I suspect they rarely communicate their thoughts to others.

~~~~~~~~~

We can tell that cultural defensive systems are involved by the emotional intensity of discussions about the Great Acceleration. Many climate change deniers are angry at "alarmists." They are not merely bored or in disagreement; they are contemptuous and furious. Contrast this with your own responses to conversations that you disagree with but do not find alarming.

Sometimes climate change deniers harass those who would help them see the situation clearly. At an Earth Day event in

Lincoln a middle-aged man walked around bullying workers at their booths. He demanded to know if we owned cars and then hurled insults at us if we said yes. His red face and his yelling spoke to his own denial and resistance.

When people discuss less emotionally threatening topics, they can afford to disagree more amicably. We may disagree about a local bond issue of limited import, such as funding a holiday parade or revising an arcane aspect of the city charter, but we are not physiologically agitated by the topic. We may not be bicyclists, but the idea of funding bike paths doesn't tend to make us hate those who disagree with our point of view. Yet when people react to talk of man-made climate change, their intensity reveals the strength of their fears.

Psychological research on cognitive dissonance shows that the more profound the threat the more rigorously it is denied, as in, "No, of course that sound couldn't be an avalanche." This indeed seems to be happening on a mass scale in our country. For example, Gallup polls show that in 2007, 50 percent of conservatives believed that global climate change was already happening. By 2010, less than 30 percent of conservatives believed this. Progressives who believed we were experiencing global climate change remained a steady 70 percent in 2007 and 2010. But even this is noteworthy. There is a rapidly growing body of evidence that change is occurring. What do the 30 percent who don't believe in global climate change think is happening?

Agnotology

Robert Proctor, a professor at Stanford, coined a new word, "agnotology," for the study of ignorance that is deliberately manufactured or politically generated. In a 2009 interview with *Wired* magazine, Proctor said, "People always assume that if they don't know something, it's because they haven't paid attention or haven't yet figured it out. But ignorance also comes from people literally suppressing truth—or drowning it out—or trying to make it so confusing that people stop caring about what's true and what's not."

For example, ExxonMobil and Koch Industries, both companies in the fossil fuel business, have spent a great deal of money funding groups to refute scientific evidence about climate change. They target Americans who are skeptical of science and of environmentalists. It is easy to convince this population that global climate change is a hoax because they want to be convinced.

In fact, corporations and politicians often hire their own scientists and pay them to say what they want said. This kind of "science" appeared in the 1960s when the cigarette companies paid scientists to claim that smoking was not harmful. And it appears constantly today in support of fraudulent information. As the Japanese say, if you believe everything you read, you'd better not read.

NEWS from the North,
East, West, and South

Our media don't necessarily tell us what to think but they can and do tell us what to think about, simply by what they choose to cover or ignore. In America, daily news is not structured to cover complex emergencies. Generally it reports on what happened, not what might happen. Deadlines are short. TV needs good visuals.

Climate change is not a hot topic. As author Bill McKibben points out in a post on *TomDispatch.com*, in 2011, "ABC, CBS, NBC, and Fox spent twice as much time discussing Donald Trump as global warming." He documents that over the last three years, a mere ninety-eight minutes of prime-time television news was devoted to covering this global challenge. In fact, in 2011, the Sunday talk shows spent exactly nine minutes of time on climate change—all of it given over to Republican politicians focused on denying it.

Recently I have noted the paradox that the more complicated our problems become, the more slogan filled and simplistic is the discourse around these problems. Logically it would seem that complex problems call for complex and nuanced thinking, but in fact, they overwhelm people. Politicians and media provide easy and useless answers. A bumper sticker trumps an essay. "Drill, baby, drill."

Even when the news media come through, it isn't enough. Journalist Krista Tippett recently said on her radio show *On Being*, "We newscasters tell people all this dreadful news, but what do we expect them to do with it? Often our listeners are already stressed to their limits with their own situations."

Often news is delivered with no sense of proportion. A story about the trial of Michael Jackson's doctor or Beyoncé's pregnancy generates much more coverage than an international conference on shrinking polar ice. A robbery may receive more attention than the oil spill on the Yellowstone River.

To be fair, there are many high-quality journalists and publications that strive to report what's happening in the world. But for the most part, the media tell us what they think we want to know. For example, in June 2012, Americans heard much more coverage of Jerry Sandusky's trial for sexual abuse than of Rio 2012, the international conference to prevent global climate change.

Journalism uses the "Chad rule" for topics. That is, don't report on topics that don't interest most people. The thought is—how many Americans really care about the African country Chad? And how many people are losing sleep over the earth's current CO_2 levels? This all becomes a vicious circle, of course. It is hard to care about what we don't know about and difficult to inform people about what they appear not to care about.

Information becomes infotainment and truth and meaning are lost in translation. I admire people who refuse to participate in the blurring of reality. A local Jewish attorney was asked to be on a radio show to debate a Holocaust denier. He refused. He pointed out that even the debate was a form of denial: we don't debate what direction the sun rises in the morning, he said. Furthermore, to engage in a debate with the

Holocaust denier was to validate the denier's view as at least legitimate enough to deserve serious discussion. And the attorney wouldn't deign to do this.

The media have adopted this dysfunctional habit. Newscasters and talk show hosts often go to great lengths to present "both" sides of a story. But not all points of view are equally credible. Some are based on knowledge and careful study of a question. Others come from hired guns or ideologues. A climate change denier with no scientific background or bona fide research to back up his claims is not the equivalent of a climate scientist who, through the scientific method, has concluded that our climate is changing. For an honest analysis of a situation, we need the media and the talking heads to distinguish between experts and propagandists and between objective analysis and public relations.

Finally, the media outlets are not good at integrating information and connecting the dots between one story and another. For example, in March 2012, when fifteen thousand different temperature records had been broken around the country, NBC Nightly News made no mention of global climate change. Furthermore, temperatures had been far above average for over a month. Many records were broken by as much as forty degrees. After one newscaster displayed a map of the astonishing heat wave, a meteorologist came and simply explained that the jet stream was in an unusual place. While this was no doubt true, larger forces were also at play.

America's Unique Characteristics

Our geography may play a role in our cultural denial. At least until recently. Predictions of imminent doom simply have not fit the experiences of most Americans. Citizens of Pakistan, Holland, and the Maldives are concerned about the earth's environmental problems because their lives are already directly affected by rising sea levels. In much of the United States, far from islands and the poles, we have seen less evidence of rising oceans or melting ice. Of course, in 2012 we experienced record-setting rainstorms and severe droughts and floods, but the grocery stores continued to be well stocked and the roads were still drivable. People could turn on the water in their taps and the heat in their homes on winter nights. On the surface, life still looked normal.

Despite its multitudinous and significant problems, our American story continues to be one of Manifest Destiny, expanding our territory and enhancing our influence in all kinds of ways. For the most part, we continue to act as if we can prosper with little concern for our environmental future. As author Garry Cooper wrote in a *Psychotherapy Networker* article, "We Americans learned our environmental stewardship from the conquistadors."

At least in our recent era, the United States has not been a country that focused on long-term planning. Our public policies and our cultural messages encourage short-term satisfaction over longer-term goals. While we tend to be deeply kind and sympathetic with individuals we know, and even to strangers in certain categories, such as abduction victims or lost children, we are not attuned to the eventual needs of yet-unborn generations of humans or other species.

If we acted on the basis of common sense, we would employ the precautionary principle in our decision making about the earth's resources. This principle is used when facing possible risks of a catastrophe. Scientific certainty or "absolute proof" is not required before taking action. We see this principle behind installing tornado sirens, running emergency drills, or enacting laws about disposing of hazardous substances. But we don't see it now when climate change looms and the issues are most critical—our water, air, food, and arable land will be compromised if we wait for absolute proof.

Our cultural philosophy also hinders our ability to deal with our global storm. Americans emphasize independence versus interdependence and rights versus responsibilities. We tend to idolize lone rangers, mavericks, and outlaws, but we have limited tolerance for social change agents.

To add yet one more complication, Americans seem uniquely intolerant of despair. Canadian novelist Douglas Coupland refers to the United States as being a place that embraces the "culture of perkiness." Psychiatrist R. J. Lifton describes the "double lives" of many Americans, who are cheerful outside but inside struggle to cope with despair. We educate our citizens to bury pain and fear with consumer goods and expensive distractions. When we are in public, we are encouraged to put on our game face and to not be too authentic. The expression of real emotions, especially about important issues, is taboo.

Our cultural icons are strong, silent men or long-suffering and cheerful women. With the exception of Quaker meetings, therapy, and AA, we have few cultural traditions for truth telling. And we have many ways of silencing dissent and despair.

A New Divide

I am old enough to remember a time in America when everyone read the same media: *Time, Look, Newsweek,* and *Life*. And we all listened to and respected the same television commentators: Walter Cronkite, Edward R. Murrow, and Howard K. Smith. I remember when talk about politics, even though heated, didn't feel personal and hateful.

But today, it seems as if our country is approaching the kind of tragic polarization that we had just before the Civil War. We are not yet fighting with weapons, unless we consider information and big money weapons, but we are fighting with ideologies. Conservatives and progressives are deeply entrenched in their belief systems and don't give much ground to people with opposing views. And both sides of this new divide listen to different radio and television shows and read different information. The facts and evidence they start from are not the same. They are also unlikely to have many friends who think differently than they do. We are becoming an increasingly split country, unable to solve problems because we cannot appreciate differences and negotiate calmly. To quote Abraham Lincoln, "A house divided against itself cannot stand."

Once I was walking with my friend Lara, who is a conservative Republican. She told me that the week before, a woman she had been friends with for twenty years broke off the relationship because she could not tolerate being friends with a conservative. Lara is a shy woman who would never impose her political views on anyone, and in fact, she had never even discussed politics with her now cut-off friend. Lara continued by saying that her husband's family had a reunion coming up, and that she and her husband were the only conservatives in the family. She said, "It's hard to go to these reunions and hear the way the family talks about Republicans. We keep our mouths shut." Then she started to cry and said, "Most of our friends are university professors and progressives. We feel lonely and isolated these days."

In recent years, many pragmatic problems—fluoridation, conservation, immigration, and climate change—have been recategorized as political ones. Our country's polarization around ideologies has distorted issues and made fixing many problems impossible.

An example of this senseless polarization comes from our local newspaper, which runs a column on sustainability and green practices. This column is written by members of Lincoln's Green by Design group, which works for goals such as more efficient use of infrastructure, green building standards, limited sprawl, and more bike paths. In 2011, a local man who belongs to Freedom Advocates protested the Green by Design column. The Freedom Advocates, an ultraconservative Web-based group, considers education about the environment to be indoctrination. The group's objectives include informing the populace about threats to freedom and encouraging them to safeguard their rights. Its website states, "Policies, procedures, and laws enacted by governmental and non-governmental agencies in the name of diversity, community, and the earth are diminishing individual liberty, degrading ecology, and threatening human life and happiness across America." Because of pressure from Freedom Advocates, the paper has printed negative anti-green columns alongside the green columns.

When practical problems fall victim to ideologies, logic flies out the window. As John Hansen, president of the Nebraska Farmers Union, told me, "It's virtually impossible to reason someone out of a position they were never reasoned into."

Pessimism

An NBC/*Wall Street Journal* poll for December 2010 found that the percentage of Americans who were optimistic was at an all-time low. Over 70 percent of Americans thought the country was going in the wrong direction. They sensed a declining middle class and felt frustrated and angry with their government and all other institutions.

This poll suggests we are losing that most American of qualities—optimism. But who needs a poll to tell us that? I can see it on the faces of everyone I meet. The country we live in turns out to be more fragile than we thought. Governments can be bought, democracy can be eroded, and lies can drown out the truth.

That poll made me think of Apollo 11 and the first moon landing in 1969. Like most Americans, I watched it on television. The screen flashed images of NASA engineers. Rows of

young men in ties and white shirts fervently followed the astronauts' every move. Their faces radiated delight and pride.
The television newscasters didn't try to hide their amazement.
All of us felt astonished and proud of what we were seeing. We
watched with bated breath as the astronauts planted an
American flag on the moon. We felt we were the best country
in the world and that we could accomplish anything. Even the
sky was not the limit.

Today that moment seems far away indeed. What happened to the whole concept of American efficacy and can-do
spirit?

In our disordered world run by giant corporations, it is
hard for people to feel that they matter or that they have any
power. We are advised to pamper ourselves, to splurge, to
binge, and to party, but we are not urged to act in ways that
would enhance our power as citizens.

Many people have empowerment and narcissism confused.
Narcissistic behavior, in the absence of an awareness of our
common humanity and shared needs, is selfish. People who
believe freedom is the ability to act on impulse do whatever
they feel like doing. "If I want to drive an enormous gas guz-
zler, that is my right." In fact, that kind of freedom makes
individuals slaves to their own whims and urges.

Most of us deeply believe in our country's best ideas—
participatory democracy, the Bill of Rights, the Constitution,
the Marshall Plan, free libraries and public education, and
national parks. We don't want to lose our country and we
grieve when we ask, "How can this beautiful place and this
powerful idea of democracy be so broken? How did the good
slip away so silently?"

We share beliefs in justice, fairness, and responsibility. We have a heritage of activists, grassroots organizers, and revolutionaries. And a new crop is coming. A University of Utah student named Tim DeChristopher was arrested in 2008 for unauthorized bidding on oil and gas leases in order to stop oil companies from despoiling the land. His civil disobedience was in the tradition of Henry David Thoreau, who refused to pay his taxes to support what he considered an unjust war. In his trial in 2011, DeChristopher appealed to a higher authority than the law—the moral imperative to care for the earth and future generations. He was found guilty and sentenced. When this happened, he looked the judge in the eye and said, "This is what love looks like."

Although we cannot return to the past, we can learn from it. Americans have a diverse history and enormous cultural resources. The indigenous peoples of our country have a strong and sustainable land ethic. On the Great Plains the Pawnee, the Omaha, the Ponca, and other cultures lived in harmony with the land and the animals. As Lakota holy man Black Elk said, "Until the white man came, the sacred hoop of life was unbroken."

Almost two centuries ago, Thoreau asked, "What's the good of a fine house if you don't have an acceptable planet to put it on?" America is the land of Pete Seeger, John Muir, Rachel Carson, Julia "Butterfly" Hill, Winona LaDuke, and Terry Tempest Williams. Many people are already working to navigate our global storm. And we have many institutions in place, from the Departments of Energy and Interior to natural resources districts and zoning councils, that could be of great value if properly managed.

Cultures, like individuals, have their unique gifts and flaws. They also have value systems, blind spots, and a long list of consistent mistakes and common heroic actions. Often the gifts and the flaws are intricately related, and only a matter of degree may separate a positive from a negative characteristic. For instance, the great American gift of an entrepreneurial and curious spirit has given us many wonderful cultural products, inventions, and institutions. On the other hand, this same spirit has trapped us in an economic cycle dependent on ever-expanding growth and exploitation of the earth.

Just as healthy individuals somehow manage to maximize the development of their gifts while limiting the damage their flaws cause in their lives, cultures also have this opportunity. America contains multitudes. Within its vast complexities, we can find an array of resources, human and otherwise, that could allow us to move forward into a fairer, more sustainable world.

AWARENESS
TO ACTION

FOUR

Learning to Swim

Awareness, Pain, Acceptance, and Action

*You have made me cross the good
road and the road of difficulties. And where
they cross, that place is holy.*

BLACK ELK

*To live is to roll up your
sleeves and embrace trouble.*

NIKOS KAZANTZAKIS, *ZORBA THE GREEK*

One night a few years ago, I slept in a tent with three of
my grandchildren. Kate was six, Aidan was four, and
Claire was two. Claire and Aidan were blissfully happy. They
snuggled and listened to the sounds of the cicadas and night
birds. Meanwhile, Kate kept telling me she was scared and
that she wanted to sleep in the house. Stupidly I chided her
for her fears. I asked, "Kate, you are the big sister and the old-
est. Why can't you be as brave as your sister and brother?" She

wailed, "Nonna, they are little. They don't know enough to be scared."

These days I often feel like Kate did that night. I know too much about deforestation, nuclear power plants on fault lines, our tainted food supply, and our collapsing fisheries. Sometimes I wish I didn't know all these things, but if we adults don't face and come to grips with our current reality, who will?

Still, sometimes it seems the reward for being conscious is fear and sorrow. A part of me envies the people who manage to stay oblivious. I have a pretty good grasp of the science of our climate crisis, but the details of its effects still can make my stomach hurt. Once on the radio, I heard a park ranger report about the bears in Yellowstone. He said that their behavior was changing. For the first time in anyone's memory, bears actually were running toward the places where they heard gunshots. The ranger said this was because they were so famished that they'd risk being killed by hunters in order to reach their kill site. He explained that the bears no longer had their traditional foods because global climate change had destroyed so much habitat and diversity in the park. That story made me feel crazy sad.

We can deal with our cultural and environmental crises only after we deal with our human crises of trauma, denial, and emotional paralysis. This will require that most difficult of all human endeavors, facing our own despair. This involves waking from our trance of denial, facing our own pain and sorrow, accepting the world as it is, adapting, and living more intentionally.

With acceptance of reality, we can integrate information

and act with awareness and intentionality. This leads to resilient, and even transcendent, coping. While I'll be discussing
our reactions to the traumatic information about the fate of
our planet, the process we'll explore fits virtually any experience that involves facing the truth with eyes unclouded by
illusion.

Awareness and Pain

In almost all spiritual traditions, suffering is a portal to awakening. Barbara Bradley Hagerty sums up research on spiritual development in her book *Fingerprints of God*. She writes,
"Brokenness stands out as the most likely trigger for spiritual
experience."

The cure for the pain is the pain. Unprocessed pain almost
always leads to something much worse than pain. Opening
ourselves up to our emotional reactions to that world and allowing ourselves to feel the gamut of emotions that opening
inevitably produces is the beginning of a movement toward
wholeness and healing. This can produce energy, focus, and a
sense of urgency. To quote Bob Dylan, "Behind every beautiful thing is some kind of pain."

Coming out of the trance of denial is painful. But crises
offer us opportunities to rethink our lives. The best thing
about despair is that it wakes us up. We can see the world
more clearly and open to new possibilities. We can deepen our
own sense of meaning and increase our compassion and connection to others. And we can find new joy in the ordinary.

Often in retrospect, our worst moment becomes part of a process that leads to our best moments.

The capacity to be strong and the capacity to be vulnerable are one and the same. For example, anger that is not skillfully dealt with can lead to aggression against the self or others. Skillfully managed, anger becomes energy that can be used to change one's own circumstances and the world.

In the Western consciousness, emotion has had a bad rap as the opposite of reason and good judgment. But psychological and neurological research reveal that emotion is the primary organizing force for human beings. It is what has enabled us to survive, form families and groups, and develop morality and empathy. The six basic emotions—joy, surprise, shame, anger, fear, and sadness—can all trigger effective responses to what is happening around us.

Psychologist James Pennebaker posits that traumatic experiences do not cause illness. Instead, keeping secrets and being unable to communicate about traumatic information— even to one's self—is what makes people physically and mentally sick. In fact, when people begin to link events, give them meaning, and communicate their experiences with others, they rapidly move toward health and develop good coping skills, regardless of what happened to them.

One of Dr. Pennebaker's main assignments to his clients who are struggling with any kind of trauma is to keep a journal and write daily about their inner experiences. Clients who do this and give themselves permission to describe their entire emotional status improve more quickly than clients who do not.

Other research also shows that humans function in more

healthy and realistic ways when they acknowledge their emotions. For example, in one study, college students were shown troubling images. The students in one group were asked to name the emotions they experienced as they looked at these images. Those students' brains were measurably calmer than the brains of the students who were not articulating their emotions.

One friend of mine said, "When I think about global climate change, it makes me feel so sad, my despair seems fatal." Psychologist Jaak Panksepp has a term, "primal panic," to refer to emotional flooding when we feel our core being is threatened. This flooding can shut us down emotionally and keep us from thinking well or responding accurately.

Awareness of our global storm often triggers primal panic. Oftentimes, because we don't know how to respond, we don't respond. And in response to our shock and numbing, we develop what psychologists call "learned helplessness."

A naturalist told me that there is no such thing as a tame snake. She said that when we see a docile snake being handled at a zoo or snake show, it means that the snake has been so continually handled and stressed that it is absolutely out of adrenaline. Its alarm system no longer triggers any arousal. How many Americans can be described this way?

Acceptance

Acceptance is the end of our argument with reality. Once we face the facts, no matter how disturbing they are, we feel calmer and less crazy. Erik Erikson defined clarity as "the capacity to fear accurately." It is an excellent catalyst for the alchemy of healing.

Bill McKibben writes that to solve our problems, "We need to see clearly. No illusions. No fantasies, no melodrama." In the process of healing, many people remember the moment when the scales fell from their eyes and they faced their fears, breathed deeply, and sensed that something within them had changed direction.

Environmentalists have a word for the realization that our planet is in urgent and serious trouble. They call it the "oh, shit" moment. Healthy people accommodate to this moment in a variety of ways. Whatever emotions we feel are the right emotions for us.

This time of awakening is a time when we want to show others and ourselves great mercy. If our problems were simple we would have figured things out long ago. If we wonder whether we can cope with the awareness, we are in good company. Everyone wrestles with that question. But a surprisingly large number of people manage to move beyond despair and anger into something stronger and more beautiful. Many humans know that when problems are too big to face, the best solution is to grow bigger.

Those of us who have spent time on a dialysis or oncology treatment unit have seen people access their bravest and kindest selves and share their sorrows and their hope with each other. My husband sometimes took his father Bernie to the hospital for his chemotherapy for prostate cancer. The chemo room was a surprisingly convivial place. People knew and cared about each other. Bernie always got hugs and laughter.

People listened well and took turns bucking each other up. Birthdays and holidays were celebrated, and when something terrible happened, as it often did, people acknowledged it, but kept on working to nurture and encourage the ones who were left.

Action

Action is the natural and healthy result of acceptance. Knowing that plastic water bottles are polluting the planet, we can switch to reusable bottles. Accepting that gas guzzlers make an enormous carbon footprint, we can forgo an automobile or drive a more fuel-efficient car.

Duane, a local lobbyist for environmental causes, illustrates an example of the process of awareness, acceptance, and action. For many years he had worked as a lobbyist for the railroads and the fossil fuel industry. During this time, he observed that few people in government were protecting our local resources or representing the needs of ordinary citizens. He also realized how much we could lose if no one was paying attention.

After a particularly dismal day at the legislature, he was disgusted and, as he put it, "I decided to switch sides and work with the good guys." He left his job and eventually became director of the Nebraska Wildlife Federation, where he has been watching out for our state's ecosystem ever since.

Maria's awareness-to-action process began when she was a young girl. At an outdoor storytelling event, she stepped forward to talk about a childhood memory. She spoke about loving the big tree in her backyard when she was a girl. From her bedroom window, she observed the birds and squirrels who lived in its branches. But the tree had to be cut down. Maria feared for the animals. Where would they go with their homes destroyed? She was helpless to save the homes of those particular birds and squirrels, but she promised herself that when she grew up, she would try to save all the animals she could. Now, as a university student, she is studying biology and devoting her time to environmental work.

Facing the Storm Together

The most effective way humans deal with emotional pain they cannot handle is to turn toward other people. Psychologists have demonstrated through research that people who are holding hands can tolerate more pain, both physical and emotional, than people who are not holding hands.

Last year a friend of mine was in a bicycle accident and broke his femur. Chris was hospitalized and his doctors drilled in five-inch screws to hold the bone together. The first night he was thrashing about in agony. Waves of grief and loneliness washed over him. All at once he sensed a nurse had entered his room.

He watched his left arm rise like that of a drowning man sinking below the waves. He didn't understand quite what he was asking for, but the nurse knew. She hurried to his left side and with both hands rubbed his forearm. Instantly he felt the pain subside and he felt less alone in the bleak darkness. Someone was with him and Chris relaxed. He had received what he most needed—a connection with another human being.

One of our most effective coping skills is simply sticking together. In a 2011 *New Yorker* article called "Social Animal," David Brooks writes, "Research over the past thirty years makes it clear that what the inner mind really wants is connection . . . Joining a group that meets just once a month produces the same increase in happiness as doubling your income."

Humans have known for a long time the pleasures of groups. Five hundred thousand years ago, we didn't wander about alone, looking for roots or animals to kill. We foraged with our own kin and clan. At night, when we sat by a campfire, we did not each sit by our own campfire. In fact, that time at the end of the day, sharing roots and grubs, grooming each other's hair, laughing, and playing with the children around a fire, was probably the beginning of what we now call community. It is what has kept humans alive through the ages.

~~~~~~~~~~

One chilly October night my daughter's women's group came over for a discussion of the ideas at the core of this book. When they were in their twenties, the women had all lived in big cities, but now, for a variety of reasons, they found themselves working in Lincoln. Even after a long workday, Sara, Jenny, Meghan, and Tiffany were a lively, talkative group.

We sat down by the fire with wine and snacks. I said, "I promise we don't have to talk about our climate catastrophe for two hours. Even ten minutes will be helpful to me." They all looked relieved. Jenny said, "That's good. I remember a night when Sara and I talked about these issues and we totally freaked out. Our conversation just got gloomier and gloomier and, in the end, we vowed never to talk about it again."

I asked how often the women thought about our climate crisis. They all answered, "As little as possible." They already had enough to worry about and they didn't know what to do with their thoughts and emotions. They all realized the gravity of our global storm, but they worked not to think about it. I asked when they did think about it and what they thought.

Meghan said, "I think about population growth when I drive across the country. I see places that used to be farmland all gobbled up by suburbs, malls, and industrial parks. Soon I won't be able to see any green space between towns, any pastures or hay fields. The landscapes I love will not exist anymore. I wonder—how much space per person will there be when we have ten billion people?"

"Maybe I think of it once every couple of weeks," Jenny said, wrinkling her nose in disgust.

Sara said, "I just can't stand to think about it, so I don't."

Tiffany told us, "I am teaching my son to be a global citizen. I talk to him about recycling and not wasting water or electricity."

Jenny looked surprised and responded, "I can't even imagine discussing this with my kids."

We talked about our natural human tendency to avoid information that upsets us. Meghan said sadly, "I think we are the only animals who experience guilt." The others readily agreed.

Jenny said, "It all seems so hopeless. What is the point of thinking about it?"

Sara said, "I am overwhelmed with my first year of teaching. By the time I get the baby down and finish my housework, I fall into bed myself."

None of these women saw themselves as change agents. Sara admitted, "I am willing to try to make good choices, but I can't commit my life to these issues. I had time for that in my twenties. Now I want to take action, but I don't want to be an activist."

I reminded her that she was on the board of a nonprofit that promotes outdoor educational experiences for children. I said, "I consider that a healthy response to our current crisis."

In spite of their guilt and desire to avoid the topic of global climate change, these women turned out to be doing a great deal to help. Their lists included using cloth bags at the grocery store and reusable water bottles, recycling, going paperless to save trees, and shopping for green products and local organic foods. Jenny said, "If I use plastic bags, I rewash and reuse them over and over until they fall apart." I laughed and said, "Wow. I never even thought of that." We all agreed none of us could do everything, but we were doing many things and maybe could do a few more.

As we talked, it was clear to me that this group experienced both avoidance and acceptance. Also, in some ways, these women were acting daily on behalf of the environment. Yet they gave themselves little credit for these actions.

All the women did what they could, even if it required a little extra money and time. These were the key issues—money and time. Organic, locally grown food costs more than standard supermarket fare and driving across town to shop for greener products isn't always possible.

The women agreed that every purchase offered an opportunity to feel engaged in good work. Jenny mentioned that they all shopped via Groupon, an online shoppers' discount service. The women talked about their hope that more green products and goods from local stores would be on discount. They decided to contact Groupon with that request.

We talked about the concept of "regifting." It has a negative connotation—as if you're dumping something you don't want on some unlucky friend or family member. However, Sara pointed out that regifting can be positive when you pass on things you don't need to people who might like them. Meghan told of a friend from Chicago who moved to Florida and gave away all her sweaters. Jenny suggested, "If someone sends you a great book that you already own, why not regift that?"

None of the women had time for community organizing or even attending events unless those events fit in with family or friend time. However, they liked Earth Day celebrations in the park and farmers' markets. Those events made it possible for them to do good and feel good at the same time.

Sara said, "I have an idea for something we could do. Sometime this winter let's have a clothing swap." Meghan added, "I'd like to schedule a book exchange party." The group eagerly accepted these ideas.

I pointed out it was now nine p.m. on a work night. We had never stopped talking about issues around global climate change, and in the process we had done a lot of laughing and supporting of each other's situations. The women were surprised by how quickly the time had passed. While we had shared honest feelings of despair and guilt, we had also found helpful and positive ways to talk about new actions to take.

In fact, the group had experienced a collective turning and moved from avoidance to sorrow and guilt, and from there to acceptance and eagerness to work. The deadness and dread with which they had approached the topic of our global storm had been replaced by vitality and the energy to act. Jenny said that she felt better after talking about these issues, something that had never before been her experience. She added that she wanted to try to help her children understand the issues and become involved in the family's recycling.

What worked in this conversation was turning from awareness to action, and making sure the actions were compatible with the lifestyles of the women. The most important lesson from this meeting was that there are ways to talk honestly about our climate crisis and not stay mired in despair. It often exits the room when people talk about getting to work.

Transcendent Response

All problems are psychological,
but all solutions are spiritual.
THOMAS HORA

This turning from trauma to acceptance to action can lead to post-traumatic growth syndrome. For example, James Campbell, a psychologist and author of *Hostage: Terror and Triumph*, wrote that the hostages he interviewed often mentioned the benefits of being hostages. They reported, "It got me rethinking things. Life is finite. Let's not waste it. Am I living the way I should be?" Or, "I am going to shift my priorities and spend more time with people I love."

My schoolteacher daughter gave her writing students this assignment: take something you consider incredibly ugly, and write about it in a way that turns it into something beautiful. In a sense, that is what we can do with the traumatic "oh, shit" moment. We can find ways to turn our awareness into opportunities to expand our points of view and elevate our consciousness. Transcendent responses can include spiritual growth, art, music, devotion to the greater good, poetry, and bliss. What they have in common is they take us beyond our current capacities into something larger, grander, and more durable.

Transcendence comes from the Latin word for climbing across or rising above. I use it here to mean moving toward wholeness. It can be a mystical state, but also it can be something simpler, the experience of seeing things in new ways, of opening to possibilities, and of breaking old habits of thinking and behaving. Transcendent events are those that facilitate our doing what my mother called "seeing beyond the fence."

W. S. Merwin, poet laureate of the United States from 2010–11, is a shining example of a person who has faced the hardest truths and found a way to respond that is transcendent. He is dealing with his own global anguish by both taking action and finding bliss.

During his tenure as poet laureate, Merwin came to Omaha to speak. As I watched him walk onto the stage in the stooped, slow way of the old, I thought that he looked too frail to be traveling. But when he spoke to us the years fell away. His voice was strong and resonant, his eyes sparkled, and his ideas were fresh and deeply original.

Merwin lives in Maui in a home surrounded by acres of tropical rain forest that he painstakingly replanted after its devastation by logging, agriculture, and erosion. He told us that he had been reluctant to accept the position of poet laureate. He preferred to be in Maui with his wife, his dog, and the trees, but, he said, "I had some points I wanted to make. This job gave me a chance to speak for the earth."

Merwin talked about what he called "our possible genetic temperament to self-destruct." He traced our attitude of dominion to the beginnings of agriculture. He argued that settling down in permanent places gave us the "illusion of possession." That fateful moment in our hominid history set us up for our downfall.

Merwin continued, "In the four hundred years since we Europeans arrived on this continent, we have nearly clear-cut the great North American forests, killed ninety million beavers, and wiped out hundreds of wild species including the buffalo and the passenger pigeon." He concluded with great sadness, "Now we are losing a species a minute and it isn't even in the newspapers."

Merwin read some poems he'd composed that gently advocate for another way of being that doesn't involve dominion. He believes that all species are created equal and that while he may choose to kill a mosquito, he is not that mosquito's superior. Nor does he believe that humans are the most intelligent species. What he does value in humans is our ability to live life on many different levels. He reveres what he calls "our not knowing." He spoke of the many kinds of wisdom humans have that are beyond conscious thought—how to comfort a child or interact with a dog or protect ourselves from a cloudburst. He said, "I have with me all that I do not know. I have lost none of it."

Merwin didn't speak of optimism or pessimism. He spoke of coping. He said, "We may not be able to change culture but we can change ourselves." He spoke of living in a state of "tragic exultation," filled with the wonder of the world in all its beauty, terror, and intensity. And he said, "On my last day on earth, I would like to plant a tree."

Group Transcendence

Disasters offer humans the chance of transcendence. They give us an opportunity to grow into bigger selves. We find new chances to help others and to define ourselves in more meaningful ways. In *A Paradise Built in Hell*, Rebecca Solnit describes the extraordinary communities that emerge after disasters such as the earthquake in Haiti or Hurricane Katrina. Contrary to the messages of disaster movies, most people do not panic and act selfishly. They rise to the occasion, build soup kitchens and health stations, and find shelter for the displaced. Solnit writes that after disasters, "Transcendence sneaks in everywhere as a survival response." She also points out, "The prevalent human nature in disaster is resilient, resourceful, generous, empathic, and brave." In fact, her research demonstrates that working for the collective good helps people through disasters.

Crises often strengthen social bonds. Researchers S. E. Taylor and L. C. Klein have shown that when humans are in danger they are much more prone to befriending behavior than fight-or-flight behavior. Collective suffering can lead us into fear, conflict, and isolation or it can foster the growth of moral imagination. We can join a community of sufferers who "tend and befriend."

Over the course of centuries, in all times and places, adaptive humans have responded to danger by acknowledging it and then acting together for the common good. We seem to know instinctively that we are stronger when we stick together. Over and over, the historical record shows us that, when the going gets tough, the tough take care of each other. Think of the Chilean mine disaster or of the Londoners during the Blitz in World War II as just two examples.

Just as countries can experience collective traumas, they also can manage the occasional transcendent breakthroughs. One example of this is the way the world community dealt with the hole in the ozone layer caused by fluorocarbons. This alarming problem, documented by solid evidence, had to be solved for life on earth to continue. And it was. In 1978, governments and businesses worked together to eliminate fluorocarbons in aerosol cans and other products. Today the hole in the ozone layer is disappearing. Scientists believe it will be back to its ideal level by midcentury. This happened because governments and corporations all over the world worked together to stop an impending catastrophe. This story is important because it shows us that global change is not only possible, it has actually happened.

When I think back to a time when Americans have faced a crisis and dealt with it adaptively, I think of the 1930s—the Dust Bowl and the Great Depression. The Dust Bowl was a man-made ecological crisis. During an unusually wet period, people on the Great Plains plowed the prairie and cut down trees. That left the land vulnerable to erosion and high winds. Then a cycle of drought and dust storms triggered an environmental collapse in great swaths of our country. While the land was mistreated and overutilized, we also experienced the ruin of our financial system. There was plenty of money in the country, but it was all in the hands of a few people. Ordinary citizens were bereft and left on their own to scramble to survive.

Yet people would show up at farm auctions to make sure no one bid on their neighbor's land or equipment. When necessary, they took in each other's children. They worked together and shared their limited resources. And as the times grew tougher, every little town had its Saturday night dances. People wore out their shoes dancing to songs that grew bubblier and more joyful as the hard times became more entrenched.

Given the fix we were in during the Depression, it's amazing that we righted our ship of state. Good governance, jobs programs and other social programs, and new laws to redistribute wealth kept people alive until the rains and the jobs returned. Lots of people contributed to make the country viable once again. Franklin Roosevelt appointed talented, competent people to manage farm and land policies and many sustainable approaches to land management emerged. Farmers planted windbreaks and changed the way they plowed. They learned to rotate crops and let the land lie fallow and recover from plantings.

There is a sense in which, like my grandchildren, all of us

are camping outdoors in a big tent. Some of us are more aware than others, and many of us feel at times that we know too much. The cure for knowing too much is not knowing less, but rather understanding what to do with the information we have. As my own story in the next chapter will show, it is about accepting the truth, and finding within that truth actionable intelligence for one's self. When I figured out what I could do, I stopped being so scared.

FIVE

Finding Shipmates

Our Coalition,
Nov. 2010–May 2011

My journey began in the cataclysmic spring of 2010. The earth was experiencing its warmest decade, its warmest year, and the warmest April, May, and June on record. Pakistan hit its record high (129 degrees), as did Sudan (121 degrees) and Saudi Arabia and Iraq (both 126 degrees). For the first time in human memory, lightning ignited fires in the peat bogs of Russia and these fires spread to the wheat fields farther south. As doctors from Moscow rode to the rescue of heat and smoke victims, they fainted in their un-air-conditioned ambulances.

All over the world, crops withered and workers dropped from heat exhaustion. Livestock died from heat and rare frogs in the Amazon rain forests disappeared. Our planet and all living beings seemed to be gasping for breath.

In Nebraska, after weeks of "hundred-year" rains, much of my state was declared a flood disaster area. In July, the heat index in Lincoln reached 115 degrees for several days in a row. Policemen wore cold packs under their bulletproof vests. All summer our local newspaper carried stories of environmental tragedies—the BP oil spill in the Gulf of Mexico and floods in Kashmir, China, and Pakistan, as well as floods in the American cities of Nashville, Milwaukee, and Oklahoma City.

In July, I read Bill McKibben's *Eaarth,* in which he argues that the earth as we used to know it already has vanished. He postulates that we now live on a new planet, Eaarth, with a different climate and a rapidly changing ecology. He writes that without immediate action our familiar ways of life will disappear, not in our grandchildren's adulthoods, but in the lifetimes of middle-aged people alive today. We don't have fifty years to save our environment; we have the next decade.

McKibben cites a great deal of alarming information from the Intergovernmental Panel on Climate Change (IPCC) Fourth Assessment Report in 2007. The report's most startling conclusion was that scientists had underestimated the damage caused by climate change. The effects of our elevated CO_2 levels were arriving a century earlier than predicted. That is, they are arriving now.

None of my reading about the environment had quite prepared me for the bleakness of *Eaarth.* I couldn't stop reading it, though I hated what I was learning. When I finished it, I felt shell-shocked. For a few days, all I could feel was despair. Everything seemed so hopeless and so over.

I teared up when I looked at flowers or listened to the flickers and kingbirds that nested near our home. When I picked raspberries with my grandchildren, I felt my heart breaking two ways at once—for the children's beauty and for their vulnerability.

I thought about all the care we lavish on these children. We make sure they eat healthy foods and brush their teeth with safe toothpastes. We examine and treat every little bug bite or scratch. We spend hours reading them books and teaching them everything from how to make guacamole to how to find, cut, and polish rocks. And yet, we—all the grandparents in the world, including myself—haven't worked hard enough to secure for them a future with clean air and water and diverse, healthy ecosystems. What is wrong with us? Where have our hearts and minds been?

That summer, when I listened to friends talking about mundane details of life, I wanted to shout at them, "Wake up! Our old future is gone. Matters are urgent. We have to do something—now."

However, after years of being a therapist and a mother, I have learned that shouting "wake up" doesn't work. In fact, that was one of my most dispiriting realizations. I wanted desperately to preserve the world I loved, but I didn't even know how to share this fact with my closest friends.

I also realized that I wasn't doing enough. I was recycling waste and using metal water bottles. I shopped the local farmers' market and I drank shade-grown coffee. By current standards, I was being a responsible citizen. But I still felt inadequate and guilty. My efforts were in no way commensurate with the gravity of the situation.

During that time my daughter and her family came for dinner during a record-breaking rainfall. After the baby went to sleep, we watched the wind whip the pines and listened to the torrents of rain hammer our windows. Sara asked if Jim and I thought the rain was related to global climate change. Jim and I stared at each other, too confused to speak.

My wonderful daughter has the same dreams all mothers have for their children. She was already doing her best. I couldn't bear to inflict any pain on her. However, Sara was persistent in her curiosity, as was her husband. In the most positive, calm way that I could, I told them what I had recently read.

Sara was devastated. She and John bundled up the baby and quickly said good night. I could see her crying as she tucked Coltrane into his car seat. I was anguished and I wasn't sure I had done the right thing. Yet Sara was thirty-three years old. Could I really shield her from what scientific experts were telling us? Would I want to be "protected" from the truth? Wasn't it better if we faced these things together?

At this time, my despair was intolerable. I couldn't enjoy anything. My conversations with my husband quickly fell into what we call "the dumper." I was afraid to be around friends for fear I would infect them with my gloominess.

I knew I had to find a way out of my state of mind. I couldn't survive with all that awareness every minute of my day. I wanted to be happy again, to be able to laugh, and to snuggle with my grandchildren without worrying about whether they'd spend their teenage years defending a meager supply of potable water with old shotguns. I wanted hope. But I couldn't forget or ignore what I now understood.

What pulled me out of my despair was the desire to get to work. I didn't know what I was going to do, I felt unqualified for virtually everything involving the environment, but I knew I had to do something. It was unclear how much my action would benefit the world, but I knew it would help me. I have never been able to tolerate stewing in anxiety. Action has always been my healing tonic.

As suggested by McKibben, I signed up on a website called www.350.org. This organization focuses on controlling worldwide CO_2 levels. The number "350" refers to scientific calculations that 350 parts per million of CO_2 is the maximum possible amount of CO_2 in the atmosphere for a sustainable planet. By the summer of 2010, CO_2 levels were already higher than 350 ppm, but this organization was working to reverse course and return us to a sustainable CO_2 level.

I ordered multiple copies of *Eaarth* and gave them to friends who promised to read them and pass them on to other readers. I found a few takers and that allowed me to talk about our climate crisis with them. Also, I visited Indigo Bridge Books and Barnes & Noble and asked them to stock more books on our environmental crisis and display them on their front counters.

The main effect of my small actions was to energize and hearten myself. I started to be able to laugh again and to enjoy my time here on earth. When I thought about the great problems we were facing, I realized I wanted to do even more. Thinking about doable activities felt better than worrying about things I couldn't control.

Then, in the fall of 2010, I read in the newspaper that the corporation TransCanada planned to build a two-thousand-mile pipeline across North America. The Keystone XL pipeline was slated to travel from Alberta to the Gulf of Mexico, across Nebraska's Sandhills. It would carry a load of crude oil, extracted from tar sands, across the Ogallala Aquifer and most of the major river systems west of the Mississippi.

Already, the tar sands development had been an ecological disaster for Alberta. The original Keystone pipeline, which connects Alberta to refineries in Illinois and a storage depot in Oklahoma, suffered fourteen leaks during its first year of operation. This kind of spillage with the proposed XL pipeline could devastate ecosystems in the Great Plains and risk compromising our nation's water supply.

I had trouble breathing as I struggled to absorb this information. As I realized some of the effects of this possible pipeline, I once again spiraled downward.

My anger and despair were deeply personal. My great-grandparents had homesteaded in the Sandhills and I grew up in a small town in western Nebraska. As a professional musician, my husband Jim had played gigs all over the state. We loved the peaceful landscapes, the open skies, and the western towns with beautiful names—Broken Bow, Rushville, Broadwater, Laurel, Lodgepole, and Valentine. We had canoed the Loup, Niobrara, and Dismal Rivers and spent summer nights camping in the Sandhills under the stars. That something I loved so deeply could be violated was upsetting enough, but, in addition, the article said that the proposed pipeline would come within ten miles of my son's home along the Platte River. If there were a leak or spill, it would flow into my grandchildren's drinking water.

Organizing a Group

The intensity of my emotions around the planned TransCanada pipeline required me, a reluctant activist, to become more involved. I invited my friend Brad, a soft-spoken organic gardener, and my friend Marian, from nearby Spring Creek Prairie, to my house to discuss what we could do to stop TransCanada from shipping tar sands sludge through our state.

We met over soup and artisan sourdough. I wanted the event to be more like a party than a meeting. I assumed that my friends were like me—too busy already and tired at the end of a workday. They would only return if they were relaxed and having fun.

We shared what little we knew about the pipeline and talked about people in our community who might be interested in joining our cause. We agreed that for our next meeting, in a week, we would invite anyone we knew who might want to jump on board.

Eight people came to that next meeting. Mitch was a young, clean-cut guy from the mayor's office. Jane, director of a political nonprofit called Bold Nebraska, had driven in from Hastings, leaving her two daughters, Kora and Maya, at home with her husband. She was a commanding, articulate woman dressed in a stylish outfit and cowboy boots. Malinda, her Lincoln assistant, arrived with yard signs and bumper stickers that said "Stop the XL Pipeline." Like all the young people that eventually joined our coalition, Malinda had plenty of enthusiasm and gumption.

Ken, a tall, skinny, tired-looking lobbyist for the Nebraska

Sierra Club; Duane, the director of the Nebraska Wildlife Federation; and Tim, the director of Nebraskans for Peace, came, too. Tim had helped organize 350.org of Omaha and was working with our power districts on ways to increase the amount of clean energy we have in our state.

After introducing ourselves to each other, we began to compare notes. Jane had been talking in the kitchens of ranchers and farmers along the proposed route. She told us that TransCanada had been bullying them into selling easements. One rancher told her that the land in the Sandhills could not recover from the digging of an oil pipeline. His grandfather had plowed a furrow to stop a prairie fire a hundred years ago. Since then, every generation of his family had tried unsuccessfully to restore the land.

"The pipeline is going to destroy vital habitats," said Marian. "I'm really worried about the sandhill and whooping cranes."

Ken and Duane told us how TransCanada was working with state officials, lobbyists, the press, and public relations people to give support for the pipeline. Ken said, "I've never seen money washing around the halls of the capitol the way I have this year."

At this point in the discussion, we were all feeling a bit overwhelmed. To paraphrase my granddaughter Kate, we were starting to know too much.

Despite the fact that several of us were looking at our feet and could no longer speak, Tim jumped in with more bad news. He made the connection between tar sands development and rising CO_2 levels, between our local struggles and a much larger climate catastrophe.

TransCanada had assured Nebraskans that the XL pipeline would be safe. But none of us was born yesterday. Ken
recalled that in the 1980s, just before Chernobyl exploded
and spewed nuclear materials around the globe, the Soviets
had reported that it would be safe for at least a thousand
years.

We talked for a couple of hours. We were like mosquitoes
in a nudist camp—we knew what we had to do; we just weren't
sure where to begin. Fortunately, with so much work, we
could choose any area that interested us and plunge in. We
could hardly plan fast enough.

We had all come into the meeting feeling isolated, hopeless, and disempowered. But despite the grim content of our
discussion, as the night went on, we became increasingly
hopeful. This seems counterintuitive, but I think I know why
it happened. That night, we weren't just complaining and be-
moaning our situation, we were planning ways to understand
and prepare for the coming storm. And we had shipmates.

All of us were progressives who had worked for lost causes
all of our lives. None of us ever seemed to vote for a candidate
who won. We didn't think we'd win this battle, either. We had
no money, organization, or public support. But we were not
just going to lie down and surrender.

We agreed to meet again in two weeks. Most of us were
foodies, so we liked the idea of biweekly potlucks with wine.
No fast food, pizzas, or sandwiches for us. We decided to
avoid office buildings, too. We'd meet outside for picnics or in
members' homes.

We called ourselves a coalition and vowed that every meeting we would plan actions. That night, we decided that our

first action would be a rally in January 2011 on the steps of our state capitol in Lincoln.

We hugged each other good-bye under the stars. Afterward, while rinsing the dishes clean, I realized I was humming. That was something I hadn't done in a long time.

Early Actions

Between November 2010 and the spring of 2011, our group met every other week. Over chili or pesto pizzas, we charted our course. Every meeting, we heard more reports about what was happening with the pipeline. And every meeting, we planned a new series of actions that we would immediately undertake.

We tried all the ordinary ways citizens influence their representatives: we requested meetings, made calls, and wrote letters. However, we were shut out of any high-level political discussions. Everything important was happening behind the scenes and only TransCanada had access. Ken and Jane, who were spending a lot of time at the capitol, were continually frustrated by the closed-door meetings, secret agreements, and influence peddling they were seeing. Ken reported that although he had been working within our state's political system for years, he'd never seen anything this corrupt.

Nothing seemed to matter to our state politicians except making TransCanada happy. TransCanada had rented land from county commissioners along the pipeline's route in case the company wanted to store equipment. It was sending charming lobbyists and PR people to work with lawmakers. To our group, TransCanada was the devil, but a devil who showed up in a tuxedo with flowers and chocolates for the politicians of our state.

We realized that on all levels, from county to federal, to quote Will Rogers, "We had the best government money could buy." No one in our coalition felt naïve about the way money and power worked in our culture, yet even the most hard-boiled members of our group were stunned by the corruption we witnessed.

I realized that in spite of my lifelong education in civic affairs, there was still a part of me that was idealistic about government and believed that it functioned the way I was taught in high school. That idealism died as we talked about politics and the pipeline. When I thought about how rigged the game was, I was beyond anger; I was too disappointed to be angry.

Our only hope was grassroots organizing of our citizens. At this stage, Nebraskans didn't know much about what was happening. TransCanada's ads peppered the state. An "agnotologist" could have conducted research on all the misleading information coming into Nebraska.

Our citizens hadn't voted for a Democratic president since 1964. In most of the counties in the state, "environmentalist" was a dirty word. However, as our coalition discussed strategies, we realized our battles were not ideological, but rather they were about local control of resources and public health. In fact, as Jane had discovered, our first allies were the landowners who were threatened with eminent domain and the people who depended on clean water and soil to make their livings—farmers, livestock producers, and dairymen. Even the big beef packers were leery about supporting a project that could undermine their profits. They knew they couldn't sell contaminated beef on world markets.

Realizing how many surprising potential allies we had across the state gave us some hope as we planned our January rally and other actions for 2011. Usually the legislature did pretty much what it wanted, with limited public scrutiny, but this time it had overreached. Every Nebraskan, of whatever political stripe, liked to drink water. It didn't get more basic than that.

Our small group was short on resources, but we stood for values that most Nebraskans held: honesty, democracy, and taking care of the land. Methodist women's groups in small towns, agribusiness men in conference rooms, ranchers in sale barns, and poets in coffeehouses all could be recruited to resist the building of what we called the "Xtra Leaky."

Our First Big Rally

The rally that we organized on the steps of the state capitol in January was our first organized protest against the pipeline. We didn't know what to expect. The newspapers didn't announce our event and we were not certain anyone knew about it. Plus, who goes to an outdoor rally in January in Nebraska?

The Nebraska capitol building, just south of downtown Lincoln, has massive steps on the west side. Reaching high above the building is a tower topped by a gold dome, built by the sodbusters during the hard years of the Depression. On top of the dome is a statue of the Sower, our iconic state symbol, who scatters grain across the state to bless its harvest.

We met on those west steps at noon. Over a hundred people arrived. Most of them were in their twenties or sixties. People wore puffy coats and gloves, and many carried handmade signs with heartfelt statements. I recognized many of the attendees, but I was struck by the number of newcomers.

Dressed in cowboy boots and jeans, Jane led the rally. Kora and Maya distributed buttons and bumper stickers as she spoke. She was spirited, passionate, and pregnant, which was a dramatic reminder of the generations to come.

We waved signs and banners and began by singing the National Anthem. As we shivered under a statue of Abraham Lincoln, we listened to ranchers, lawyers, grandmothers, and scientists explain why the pipeline was a bad idea. The crowd applauded and whooped in agreement.

I hadn't seen faces this shining and hopeful in a long time. It wasn't clear if this event would ultimately influence our politics or our politicians. But we had succeeded in giving citizens an opportunity to voice their concerns and to meet their fellow citizens with the same concerns. That alone, in our fragmented society filled with busy people, was a start.

Afterward, shivering coalition members gave interviews to the local media and passed around sign-up sheets so that we could all stay connected. Many people walked directly into the capitol to find their state senators and ask their positions on the pipeline. I drove home chilled and hungry. And elated.

Educating Our Community

As a coalition, we felt more positive as we approached our second event. In February, several hundred people showed up on an icy Saturday at an old church by the Nebraska Wesleyan University campus. So many cars showed up that Tim and I had to stand in the street to forestall a mini traffic jam. It was my first experience of directing traffic, and I have to say, it will be my last.

During the workshop, Mitch presented a video that he and Malinda had made the weekend before in the Sandhills. One of the images in the video was of a farmer sticking a pipe into the ground and drinking the water that bubbled out, as if drinking from a fountain. Another was of a farm wife in a cotton dress digging into the ground to plant a tree. Immediately the hole she dug filled with water.

As they watched this video, people shook their heads in amazement. A few people groaned, and others gasped. Those who were not from the Sandhills had never understood how close the water table was to the surface. Until now.

A farmer from North Dakota in a worn pair of cowboy boots and a baseball cap reported that after he saw an oil geyser explode near his home, he immediately called Trans-Canada's hotline to report it. The operator put him on hold for twenty minutes, and it was a long period of time before the company was able to respond to his information. After the shutdown of the leak, the cleanup response was totally inadequate. He warned us, "Don't let TransCanada come into your state. You'll be sorry."

After the end of the workshop I spoke. I gave people ideas for projects in their own communities and talking points for conversations with their neighbors. I closed with what I hoped was an inspirational line: "No one will save us but ourselves, so let's get to work."

Afterward we had an intense group discussion. The first attendee who spoke said, "When I first heard about the XL pipeline, it made me want to throw up." Another person began to cry as he described his grandparents' home in the Sandhills. Several expressed hopelessness. An older man stood up to warn us that no matter what we did, we could never win in a battle against big oil. One man who looked like a former football player was angry and had to be restrained from a long diatribe.

"All of the emotions we've heard expressed today are totally understandable and potentially useful to our cause," I said. "Anger, for instance, can be transformed into passion. And sorrow is really a manifestation of extreme love at the thought of loss."

I continued, "By acting together, we can help each other deal with not only our reactions to the news about Trans-Canada, but we can also work to create a different balance of power in our state. We can form a strong community of people who care about protecting our resources." I quoted Jim Hightower: "Let those who say it can't be done get out of the way of those who are doing it."

By March, our group had experienced a few small successes and we were feeling stronger. At our meetings, we were laughing more. We were hopeful and excited as we talked about future goals.

We planned two significant actions for the month. Bold

Nebraska and the Sierra Club funded travel to Washington, D.C., for a delegation of citizens to talk to our representatives and to people in the Department of State and the EPA. Jane went along, even though her baby was due in April. Many of the delegates, especially the ranchers and farmers, had never actively participated in government. But after traveling together, attending two days of meetings, and testifying before congressional committees, they were on fire. Every one of our delegates came home even more deeply committed to our cause. They vowed to organize their communities and stay with our coalition to the finish.

Our First Big Party

Later that month in Lincoln, we held a benefit at the Zoo Bar. Coalition members asked their musician friends to step up and donate their music. The Toasted Ponies, the Melody Wranglers, John Walker and the Prairie Dogs, Chris Sayre and the Laddies, and the Lightning Bugs all played at the event. Senator Ken Haar, one of the few state senators fighting TransCanada, spoke to roars of approval.

The place was packed with people enjoying themselves and talking about the pipeline. We danced to Hank Williams and Van Morrison. Brad and I sat by the front door taking donations in Ben's cowboy hat. Ben was a young poet and rancher whose family had homesteaded in the Sandhills and run cattle there ever since. He had come back from a cattle operation in Missouri to fight to save his family's and his neighbors' lands.

As people left, they crammed more donations into the hat and thanked us for our work. They signed up to volunteer and hauled out posters and yard signs. This event built momentum. People told us as they left, "I had no idea that this was happening. Now that I know, I want to help. What can I do?"

Surprising Allies, Unanticipated Successes

Our group was on a roll and nobody was more surprised than we were. All of us were inured to failure, but success was a little discombobulating. We were accustomed to being marginalized. But now we were riding on a powerful current much bigger than we were.

Citizens all over the state were united against our common enemies: our unresponsive state government and the big bully TransCanada. Suddenly, urban progressives were drinking coffee in the kitchens of Holt County ranchers. Republican farmers were attending strategy meetings at the headquarters of Bold Nebraska. Refugees were working side by side with college students and small-town business owners. Ken was invited to remote places that historically would have tarred and feathered anyone from the Sierra Club. He would arrive at community centers filled with people who, much to his astonishment, were on his side.

Over the next few months many newspapers in our state provided their readers with tutorials on land, water, and energy issues. TransCanada became a topic in city cafés, bars, Rotary Clubs, auction barns, and church basements. We'd never seen anything like this. Something transformative was happening, something none of us had even dared to imagine. At our meetings, we looked wide-eyed at each other. One of our most common questions was, "Can you believe this?"

During the spring of 2011, our group's emotions rose and fell like ocean waves. To our dismay and frustration, the legislature was in session but doing nothing to regulate pipelines or protect us. But we were excited to make connections with many national groups. Bill McKibben and 350.org decided to make stopping the pipeline their first priority.

Resistance to the tar sands development had started with indigenous groups on both sides of the border, especially with the Indigenous Environmental Network. The group continued its campaign with the help of us Nebraskans and many other groups.

Both the national Sierra Club and the Friends of the Earth named Nebraska a key battlefield to stop the XL pipeline. In fact, we were the only state with a solid, organized, and long-lasting resistance to TransCanada. Locally, more and more Nebraskans opposed the pipeline. Every day we read letters to the editors and editorials protesting TransCanada. An Omaha law firm had agreed to look at a class-action lawsuit against TransCanada on behalf of the harassed Sandhills landowners.

Planning a New Action

We met to discuss all of this in Tim's restored house. From his greenhouse next to the kitchen, we picked fresh lettuce, tomatoes, and herbs. As we dined on homemade bread and split pea soup, Tim opened bottles of local beer and organic wines. Brad had brought us cheese from a nearby farm and Carol had made our favorite snack—kale chips.

We began our meeting by toasting Jane and her family, including its latest member: Willa Elisabeth, born that week. By now we had many new members. One was Carol, who had donated a house so that the Bike Kitchen, a bike repair cooperative, could have a home. The group repairs bikes, then gives them to people who need transportation. Another was Nancy, a retired schoolteacher who had moved to Lincoln to help care for her grandchildren. Pippa also came on board. She was a sparkly actor and playwright. Adam had joined us. He was the young and big-hearted owner of a coffeehouse and informal community center. We also welcomed Christy, a leader of Amnesty International, and Shelly, who managed a Dippin' Dots ice cream company, to our crew. At her first meeting, Shelly said, "I didn't know I was an activist until someone asked me to be one." She came because she wanted to keep Nebraska safe and clean for her grandsons.

Our discussion that April reflected the roiling seas our small boat floated upon. We sat in a wood-paneled dining room around an oval table and talked about the State Department's unsatisfactory environmental impact study. (A group that worked with TransCanada had conducted the highly compromised and inadequate study.)

Ken said he was rounding up scientists to rebut the study's findings. Tim reported that TransCanada had bought up almost all of the airtime on television and radio, newspaper space, and public relations firms in the state just to make sure that even if our side had money to get our message out, we would have little access to vehicles of communication. At that point, our new activist Shelly said, "Whoa. I had no idea how crazy this situation was."

I lamented that the corporation had so much money that it could hire the best people for any job. It could hire lovable people and barracudas, people who would take our senators hunting or deep-sea fishing, and people who ran top-notch PR firms.

Marian had just returned from D.C. and she reported with disgust that there were signs all over the city promoting the pipeline. But she also announced that in the small town of Stuart in western Nebraska 150 people had attended our educational session. She heard a rancher tell the crowd, "I am not an activist. I am an ordinary guy. But enough is enough."

Afterward, the ranchers at that meeting said they wanted to come to Lincoln for a protest, maybe on their tractors. That energized us. We decided to host a citizens' forum in the capitol in the chamber across from the one where the legislature (the Unicameral) met. We wanted our session to be an example of what our legislature should be doing. Our proceedings would be open and democratic. We would ask scientists to testify, and all citizens would have the opportunity to be heard. We left Tim's house bolstered by our shared devotion to our cause and excited about our new action plan.

Our coalition was allowing us to turn our individual anger, fear, and sorrow into something better and stronger. Working together, we were experiencing what Nelson Mandela called "the multiplication of courage." Our support of each other during this difficult time for our state gave us a safe harbor.

And while my story is a Nebraska story, wherever you are, you, too, can find shipmates who, like you, are eager to act to help themselves feel more hopeful and to help their communities be more sustainable.

RESILIENT
COPING

SIX

Sailing On

New Healthy Normal

*Pessimism is reactionary because it makes the
very idea of improving the world impossible.*

GEORGE ORWELL

In our tempestuous times, we can be vibrant, authentic, and emotionally healthy people. In the context of our global storm, the *new healthy normal* requires the ability to move from awareness to action on a regular basis, to maintain a sense of balance, and to live intentionally. It also requires a particular kind of optimism, a connection to a community, and a world-class set of stress-reduction skills. Implied in the term "new healthy normal" is my assumption that it is not mentally healthy to sit idly by while the human race destroys its mother ship.

I consider my friends George and Sherri to be members of the new healthy normal. George has spent his life running various forms of human service programs and currently he is approaching retirement. Sherri works at a small private college. They told me that they cope with their knowledge of the world's impending fate by dealing with things as they come up. For example, they are protecting an ancient grove of trees, planting a vineyard, and restoring an old barn. In the meantime, they are connoisseurs of gratitude.

One May evening we sat on their front porch in the country and watched the goldfinches, swallows, and grosbeaks. George spoke of his worries about the diminishing number of bees in our area. They needed them to pollinate the grapevines that the family was growing on his land. He said he was concerned that life would be tougher for his sons than it was for him, and tougher still for his potential grandchildren. He said he was not sure his sons would want to bring children into this world and he could understand and accept that. He sighed and said, "I think older people have always worried about their kids, but it feels like this worry may be a new kind of deal."

Then he changed the topic to his goal of restoring a brome pasture to a natural prairie. We walked that land and tried to identify the indigenous flora. I commented on the sunset sky and Sherri said, "You know, I've never seen an ugly sky. Every time I look up it is beautiful."

We returned to their porch. As the air cooled, we could smell the dirt, the roses, and the honeysuckle. The lightning bugs came out and we could hear the droning of cicadas as the wind died down. George looked across a landscape of trees and flowers toward the ancient barn. "You know, we are the lucky ones. Not only have we been born and been able to live into ripe old ages, but also we have been able to live in green places and see the stars. No matter how down I am about the world, I feel grateful."

Constructive Awareness

Awareness is an important step in the healing process, but we need not feel conscious of our global problems all the time. Most of the time, we can live "as if" the world we know will long continue. Constructive awareness allows us to think about our global storm when we have an opportunity to make choices about our behavior. For example, when we are going to the grocery store, we can pick up our cloth bags as we walk in and pay attention to where the produce comes from and if it is organic. On the other hand, when we are at a softball game with our friends, we don't need to think about the fate of the earth.

Mother Jones said that her job was to comfort the afflicted and to afflict the comfortable. That is a useful idea for our current situation. For us to successfully cope with our global storm, some people need more awareness, but others are already painfully aware and perhaps unable even to enjoy life because of their constant sense of doom. That group might benefit from titrating their awareness the way chemists titrate certain medicines, such as the heart medicine digitalis. Too much digitalis is poisonous; however, if prescribed in small doses, it can be lifesaving. Healthy people titrate both the urgent and essential information and their emotional reactions to it. They pay attention to science and accept responsibility for their own behavior. They manage to make good choices without feeling overwhelmed too much of the time.

We all can be aware, then not aware. To respond adaptively to our environmental problems, we need to tolerate anxiety long enough to understand our situation and to organize ourselves for action. Then we can return to other topics. We can bake that peach pie or join a choir or bike along the river trail at sunrise.

Resilient people are often aware of our global storm even though they say that they rarely "think" about it. Still they show by their actions that they're engaged in protecting the earth. They are recycling, driving a hybrid, biking to work, or using cloth diapers. They have managed to be concerned for our troubled world and yet also to rest from those concerns.

My friend Chuck's thinking is an example of constructive awareness. I asked him once how often he thought about global climate change. He responded, "I rarely think about the fate of the earth. I am not in denial, but I just don't go there." He continued, "I try to live lightly on the planet. I garden, compost, and recycle. I am not a big consumer and I don't like to fly." Then he switched the topic to the TV series *Deadwood*.

Intentionality

In my book *The Shelter of Each Other*, I argued that if we just let the culture happen to us we end up rushed, stressed, addicted, unhealthy, and broke. I want to advance that argument by suggesting that we be intentional with our time and money not only for ourselves and our families but for the entire planet.

Every one of our actions has consequences. If we keep this in mind as we navigate our lives, we will see that we have many opportunities every day to act for the common good. As consumers, students, parents, employees, and neighbors, we make choices all the time. Some choices, such as selecting a regular mode of transportation, a profession, or the dwelling we inhabit, can require a great deal of effort, expense, and long-term planning. Other choices are easier. It isn't onerous to recycle newspapers or turn the thermostat down at night. It only takes a few seconds to turn off unnecessary lights or to call and cancel a subscription to a catalog or a magazine we no longer read.

Of course, some of our choices have implications for other choices. House size, energy efficiency, and location all have significant effects on our budgets and our carbon footprints. And home location has a big effect on transportation decisions. Choosing an apartment near a metro line or within walking distance to work, living near family or the children's school—all these can save commute time and help reduce our use of fossil fuels.

My friends Dave and Monique are excellent examples of this kind of intentional living. They live in Takoma Park, Maryland, with their two young daughters. Monique telecommutes thirty hours a week for a nonprofit that educates the public about global climate change. Dave drives their Prius into D.C., where he works for an animal welfare institute.

They reside in a heavily populated area, but they manage to live relatively simply and sustainably.

Monique once told me, "It is the driven of the world who have the hardest lives. They don't see their families or have time to enjoy a garden or a bedtime story. They may have money and prestige, but they are poor. True wealth for our family means the time to be patient and loving with each other, time to rest and play, and a sense that we are doing what we can to be good citizens of the earth."

Their living situation is not ideal. Dave has a long commute to his job and they are far from any truly wild areas. However, they wanted to live where Monique could do without a car and they finally located a ground-floor apartment within walking distance of a library, a school, a park, and a co-op. Monique could plant tomatoes and a few flowers and herbs in a small green space.

Monique and the girls know their neighbors and the local store owners. Most of the time they are not in a hurry. Monique said, "Not having to rush is the greatest luxury an American can experience these days."

The family has a good time on a limited budget. Monique is masterful at creating a sense of wonder and connection to the natural world. She told me, "Whenever we have dramatic weather, we walk to a local restaurant and watch the storm from their windows. We rarely go out to eat, so storm watching at a café is a double treat. I especially enjoy it during a heavy snowfall, when walking to the café is half the fun."

As they walk around town, Monique teaches her daughters the names of the trees, birds, wildflowers, and ornamental plants. She wants them to pay attention to the natural world, which will always be a solace to them, no matter what happens.

Monique said that the children, like all children since the beginning of time, enjoy foraging. She taught them how to identify poison ivy, and they search for mulberries, wild onions, and wild asparagus. They have found pawpaw (a native banana-type fruit) in a few select spots. Sometimes Monique and the girls take public transportation or rent a Zipcar and go to places where they can find mushrooms and other wild food. She told me, "Even in the city, we can always connect with the heavens. I have educated the children to just find the widest expanse of sky that they can and enjoy it."

Monique and Dave manage to savor their lives at the same time they are caring for the earth. These are the kinds of global citizens that will help us create a new world.

We can be intentional in our decisions about vacations and leisure time. Before we make our decisions, we can explore questions like, How far from home will we travel? Shall we go by bike, car, train, or airplane? Do we have closer alternatives nearby? What kind of tourism and recreation do we want to support with our choices?

Travel has always been a big source of pleasure for Jim and me and we have struggled to find the right balance between saving and savoring. Some of our happiest times have been traveling to festivals and parks. We still travel but we are experimenting with the staycation. One day a month, we go off the grid. We wake up and make one decision at a time about what we feel like doing. We don't take phone calls or look at our computers. We don't pay bills or do housework. We just enjoy whatever we feel like doing in our area. Sometimes we go out to lunch or to an art gallery. Almost always we take a long walk.

Before we experimented with the staycation, we were skeptical about how much we would like these days at home. I thought we might get bored. Jim wondered if he could avoid checking his e-mail. But after our first one, we were hooked. It turns out that they are as much fun as taking a trip and a lot less expensive. I am sure we'll travel again, but meanwhile, these staycations are giving us much of what travel gives us—relaxation, slow time, spontaneity, and escape from responsibility.

We can exercise our power of choice to create a sustainable world when we shop. Whenever we make a purchase we can ask ourselves, Can we buy it used, borrow it, repair what we already have, find a better alternative, or do without?

We can be intentional with the food we buy. We can look at the stickers on fruits and vegetables and try not to purchase anything from far away. We can cut back on beef and other meats that require a great deal of resources to produce. And, even if we aren't vegetarian, we can have meatless meals several times a week. We can purchase green products whenever possible and avoid buying endangered fish and shrimp. Sigh. This last suggestion is truly difficult for our family. Shrimp is our coin of the realm. Everyone loves it and associates it with holidays and birthdays. One of my grandson Aidan's first words was "swimp." We still buy shrimp, but more sparingly and with more care about its source.

In Western culture, we have a tendency to compartmentalize the ways we earn our living from what we call real life. Many decent people learn to check their integrity and values at the office door at eight a.m., then reclaim them at five p.m. How they spend their workdays doesn't connect to how they define themselves as people. For example, kind and conscientious parents can somehow find themselves making products harmful to children.

This kind of compartmentalization of identity, at its most extreme, is what the Nazis did. In *The Nazi Doctors: Medical Killing and the Psychology of Genocide*, R. J. Lifton interviewed Germans who had been involved in the slaughter of innocents. He concluded that many people would do anything with a relatively clear conscience as long as they could label it work. If they were obeying orders from a superior they would behave in ways they would never consider in their off-duty lives. In the early 1960s, Stanley Milgram learned this same thing with psychological studies.

I've always liked Henrik Ibsen's definition of work as "the creation of good on the planet." I've also found that the best work allows people to use all of their gifts for the common good. We could define an authentic life as one in which one's values and behaviors are congruent. That is what the Buddhists call "right livelihood," and that is the kind of work that makes most people happy.

One of psychologist Martin Seligman's early research projects involved giving students one of two assignments—they could do a good deed or they could give themselves a treat. He asked them to rate their happiness at the time and a week later. When the event occurred, the students who had done a good deed reported higher happiness scores. And a week later, these students felt even happier when they remembered their good deed than did the students who had indulged themselves. Seligman discovered that not only is philanthropic action more fun than doing something defined as pleasurable, but also that it has longer-lasting effects on happiness.

His later research revealed that the happiest workers were those who felt that they made real contributions and that their occupation was congruent with their interests and values. Many examples of this spring to mind: cooks who pride themselves on preparing healthy food, journalists who cover environmental news, or landscapers who promote indigenous, low-impact plantings. Businesspeople who care for their employees and communities and who sell services or things that help also tend to be happy people.

Research shows that acting intentionally on behalf of the future cheers people up. As Dr. Dan Siegel, a neuropsychiatrist at UCLA, teaches, "Even if the situation is hopeless, the mind is healthiest when it acts as if there is hope."

In an interview for *On Being*, immunologist Esther Sternberg talked about what has historically been called the "placebo effect." She redefined it as the brain's own healing process, which is always motivated by hope. She did not object to the word "placebo," but she said it is commonly preceded by the adjective "just." In fact, in modern medicine, the placebo effect is enormous. Sternberg cited research that shows placebos reduce pain and inflammation by up to ninety percent in patients recovering from surgery. This information is about healing the body, but as Siegel and others are discovering, hope is also very good for the mind.

Suzanne Segerstrom, in a book called *Breaking Murphy's Law*, writes that optimism is not about being positive so much as it is about being motivated and persistent. Her research found that rather than walking away from difficult situations, optimists tend to confront problems head-on. They focus on solutions and plan a course of action. She continues that when optimists are faced with uncontrollable stressors, they tend to react by building "existential resources." Her phrase "existential resources" is similar to what I mean when I write about transcendent responses.

What both of us are talking about is the phenomenon that when we face challenges that seem beyond our capacities to cope, resilient people are able to accept the difficulty of the situation and grow into people who can meet it.

Another of Seligman's findings from this field of study was that happy people are more altruistic than unhappy people. This surprised him. He had predicted that unhappy people would be more empathic for others' suffering. In fact, happy people are more generous both emotionally and financially. They have more empathy. A 2007 study by Stephanie Brown showed that altruistic people actually live longer lives. Her work with 423 old couples found that those who gave substantial support to others were more than twice as likely to remain alive in a five-year period.

In his book *The Pursuit of Happiness*, psychologist David Myers reviewed research on the relationship between money and happiness. He found that once personal income had reached a stable but rather modest level, more income didn't make people any happier. Instead, what made people happy was more time with friends and family. He concluded that happiness often involves living a simple life, consuming less, and savoring more. He cited a study that found that the less expensive recreation is, the more people enjoy it.

Americans actually rate themselves higher on happiness scales when they are gardening than when they are snow skiing or power boating.

What was once called voluntary simplicity is becoming less voluntary. Our middle class is vanishing and our spendthrift ways are dying a natural death. But involuntary simplicity is not all bad. Myers reported that many people who have less money than Americans—such as Mexicans and Costa Ricans—are much happier. All over the world in the countries with the highest happiness indices, people enjoy each other rather than products. They share a sense of community. Relationships are more important than business or "stuff."

My friend Marian is a good example of the optimistic personality that results from an intentional life. Her work at Spring Creek Prairie allows her to enjoy much of what she enjoyed as a girl. As a child on a farm, her favorite sound was that of the screen door slamming behind her in the morning. When she heard that she knew the whole world was out there waiting for her.

As a child, Marian was influenced by the TV ad campaign for Keep America Beautiful that showed an American Indian with a tear rolling down his face. She lived where she could gather arrowheads and that image was powerful to her. An article in her *Weekly Reader* suggested an experiment: take a jar and fill it with water, paper, cigarette butts, garbage, and oil, let it sit for a month, and observe what happens. She did that and, after a month, the water looked nasty. She thought, "This is what happens if we don't pay attention to what we are doing."

Marian remembers loving to catch lightning bugs with her

friends. They would catch them in jars and then pull off their abdomens and stick them on their fingers to look like rings. She loved them but she killed them. She told me there is a sense in which all of her life's work is atonement to those lightning bugs.

By now, Marian's moral imagination includes the point of view of the bluestem and the garter snake, the catfish and the bobcat. She also has been able to sustain her sense of wonder. Marian told me, "One morning I was looking at a decaying inky cap mushroom when I realized the whole thing was pulsing. It looked like a blob coming to life. I grabbed a magnifying glass and it turned out that all kinds of flies lay their eggs in the gills of mushrooms and the little larvae were all hatching. That experience woke me up for the day."

She continued, "It is a great gift to work on a prairie. Every day when I arrive, I feel like the little girl who ran outside on a summer morning, alive with happiness to discover what was going on." She laughed and added, "We already know everything if we can just remember it."

Balance

Almost everyone who is awake and conscientious right now struggles with hard choices about personal energy. People who do good work are in demand and they can easily become exhausted victims of their own kindness. Especially when we hope to avert the destruction of our planet, we can find ourselves working twenty-four/seven.

To be in balance we somehow must manage to care for ourselves and to nurture other living beings. It can mean finding the right mix of detachment versus engagement and of fun versus fervor. In Korea green tea is regarded as the perfect drink. It has all of nature's flavors—sweet, sour, salty, bitter, and pungent—in perfect balance. The balance of the tea has led to a philosophy that teaches: try to live a life that is not too arduous, not too comfortable, not too difficult, not too grandiose, and not too complicated.

When I was a girl, I worked in the office of my doctor mother. One day a teenage girl who glowed bright orange from head to foot came in to see her. While this patient was with my mother, the nurse and I speculated on what could have turned the girl orange. We thought of health problems or some kind of allergic reaction to skin cream. Neither of us had ever seen an orange-colored person.

At the end of the workday, I asked my mother what had caused the young girl's orangeness. She laughed and said, "It's a funny story." She went on to explain that the girl had read that carrots would make her lose weight and be good for her vision. So, for several months, this conscientious girl had eaten several bags of carrots a day. The carotene had colored her orange. My mother said, "I told her carrots were healthy, but only in moderation and that everything, even the best foods, must be balanced by other foods. Healthiness is in the balance."

A group at the Women's Theological Center in Boston has a motto: "We must go slowly, there is not much time." One day when I was a stress monkey, someone helped me out. At the grocery store, I was rushed and forgot to sign my check. When the cashier handed it back to me, I said, "This is what happens when I get in a hurry. It always slows me down." The carryout man was Danny, who lived in a sheltered living situation and had some cognitive limitations. However, Danny had a high emotional IQ and an A-plus character. That day he looked at me, shook his head, and said, "When I hear people say they are in a hurry, that's when I step in and tell them, 'You are gonna be okay.'"

Balancing our passions enables us to live in ways that restore ourselves and the earth at the same time. This is a traumatic decade, and our emotional reactions to the news of the day will often be intense. Likewise, we may experience an incandescent commitment to helping the world. All of the fire of our passions about the global storm must be balanced by savoring the experiences we have day by day as we move about our communities.

Savoring the World We Have

We can begin to take care of ourselves by doing what all mammals do. We can live in our bodies and enjoy the pleasures offered to us by our senses. Animals know what they need. They eat when they are hungry and sleep when they are tired. They try to stay comfortable and have fresh water to drink. They live much like their—and our—ancestors did.

We humans are happy when we engage in the most ancient and basic behaviors—being outdoors, cooking, joking, resting, looking at sunsets and stars, telling stories around a fire, and snuggling with children. Sustaining activities are easy to find. I have my own list of healing tonics, including music, meditation, walks with friends, swimming, and reading. No doubt you can make a list of your own.

Children are a great aid in both stress reduction and joy production. Many of the problems adults have—being in a hurry, not being present, multitasking, not noticing the world around them—are not problems that most children have. Children live in the now and are not conscious of time until they have been tediously educated to be. I remember a day when my five-year-old grandson called me. Aidan wanted to tell me that he had found a turtle. I was busy and, while enthusiastic, not totally present. Aidan said, "I love you, Nonna," and I responded, "I love you, too." After a moment of silence, Aidan said, "No, Nonna, I mean I love you *right now.*"

At that moment, I felt chastened, but also blissfully in love with Aidan.

Another day my friend Margie brought her dog over for a walk around the lake. When we returned to my house, Leo began rolling around in the grass. First he rolled on his back, then he lolled about on his stomach trying to have every possible inch of skin touching the grass. Margie said, "If you want to know the time, ask a dog. They always know, and they'll tell you the correct time, which is now, now, now."

What I find most sustaining is what I loved as a girl: lying down on my back and looking at the sky. That is my first memory and I hope it is my last.

Not long ago, after a rough week, I felt compelled to drive to Spring Creek Prairie Audubon Center, which is about thirty

minutes from my home. I joined a group of birders doing a
winter bird count. It was a grand experience, with long lines
of snow geese overhead, woodpeckers in the burr oaks, and a
mink ice-skating on the little pond. However, at some point, I
wanted to be alone and away from people, even the birders I
normally enjoy.

I walked alone to a sunny patch of prairie, lay on the
ground, and looked at the sky through the waving big bluestem. I imbibed the prairie. I felt the warm earth beneath me.
I smelled the moisture, the dirt, and the cereal-like aroma of
the tall grasses. I looked up through the golden seedheads at
the blue sky and the geese. I heard their calls and the wind
rustling in the grasses. As I lay there breathing as the earth
breathed, I thought, "I am getting what I most needed today."

Visiting with other human beings may be one of the most
ancient healing tonics. In the spring of 2010, when my daughter called for a dental appointment, she found out her dentist
had retired suddenly. The receptionist told her that Dr. Melvin had cancer and was already in hospice. Sara had seen this
dentist since she was three years old. Our entire family had
had Dr. Melvin in our lives at least twice a year for three decades. He had displayed the children's drawings on his bul-
letin board and given us tomatoes and squash from his garden.

He and Sara had a close relationship that included jokes
about their political differences. She was heartbroken by the
news of his illness. Like almost everyone else, my daughter
was swamped with work, but she couldn't quite forget how

much Dr. Melvin meant to her. So she called the office and asked if she could visit him and show him her new baby. The office checked and the family invited her over.

Sara took the baby and some bread and cheese and sat with her dentist for about half an hour. He had aged twenty years in the past few months. Sara handed him her baby, and Coltrane, who was normally shy around strangers, smiled and snuggled into Dr. Melvin. It was a happy occasion for all and it came about because my daughter decided to slow down, ignore her to-do list, and do what her heart felt was important and necessary.

~~~~~~~~

Adam Hintz is a member of our coalition and a person who defines the new healthy normal. He's aware, engaged, vital, and deeply connected to his family and community. At age thirty-one, he is a family man and a businessman. He is one of the owners of Meadowlark Coffee & Espresso. He is married to Anne and is the father of two young daughters, Iris and Sophia. He likes to be home with his daughters by four in the afternoon. As Adam puts it, "Everything I do, I do for them."

Adam was born in Lincoln at a hospital located across the street from his current business. His dad was a maintenance man and his mother was a homemaker. Adam said, "I learned cynicism from my dad and compassion from my mom."

When he was young, he swung from ropes and vines like Indiana Jones, his hero at the time. Like Luke Skywalker, Adam wanted to fight against the evil empire. For a while he trained himself to be Batman. He smiled and told me, "I was pretty old before I realized I couldn't be Batman. I didn't have the money or infrastructure and they don't sell Batcars."

Then he thought of becoming a Catholic priest. "I had such a love of God and I wanted to help others." However, that plan fell through because he liked girls too much. In high school, he became an atheist, but he said, "I kept my Catholic sensibilities for the sacred."

Adam found high school to be a mishmash of information with no discernible meaning. He looked elsewhere for guidance. He was a fan of grunge music, particularly Pearl Jam, whose singer, Eddie Vedder, he admired. Because of Vedder's influence, he became a vegetarian and an activist. After Vedder did an album based on Daniel Quinn's *Ishmael*, Adam read the book and all of Quinn's writing.

He now believed that our thinking in terms of dominion was the cause of our problems. He realized that humans had lived easily on the land as hunter-gatherers for most of our existence. Now we were destroying the earth with our unsustainable activities. He said, "I became so aware, I didn't know what to do with myself."

At first he was too shocked to organize himself for any kind of action, but the September 11 attacks jolted him out of passivity. His opinions about what had happened, why it had happened, and what our response should be were markedly different from those of most Nebraskans. Yet he felt he couldn't speak out. He searched for leadership to help him focus on positive goals, but he couldn't find a leader. At the time he was dating Anne, who said, "You have a great deal you should be doing, so do it. What are you waiting for?"

Adam's first real activism was to participate in local efforts to stop the war in Iraq. He joined the Coalition for Peace. He formed a little group, Prairie Zephyr, that took antiwar movies to small towns. After he showed the movies, everybody would discuss them. Not many people came, but the ones who did felt inspired by the events. He felt strongly that the Iraq War was a defining moment for the planet. He wanted to stop it and be a part of a world-changing activity, but, of course, he didn't succeed.

After the war began, Adam focused on his own personal growth. When he was driving, he listened to CDs of great thinkers. He learned to garden organically and compost. He reseeded his yard with prairie grasses and joined Bioneers and Community CROPS.

One January night in 2005 Adam and his friend Nate were playing poker when they decided to open a coffeehouse based on the principles in Quinn's *Beyond Civilization: Humanity's Next Great Adventure*. Adam told Nate he would ask his parents for some money. When he told me about this, he choked up. "I was a lazy, long-haired hippie, but my parents loaned me twenty-five thousand dollars."

Four months later, on Earth Day 2005, Nate and Adam opened Meadowlark. It is a community business with local goods and fair trade and shade-grown coffee. They keep the hierarchy to a minimum. The place is staffed by a close group of friends who share common goals. Adam explained to me, "It is always emotional when someone has to leave the job."

Adam sees the coffeehouse as his opportunity to be a community educator. He told me he tries to listen with his heart and be a role model for sustainability. He works to make every one-minute conversation with customers meaningful. For example, if someone asks what he is doing over the weekend, he might tell her that he is getting his rain barrels ready and encourage her to think about getting a rain barrel, too.

He shows educational movies at the coffeehouse, such as *The Ground Truth*, *Out of Iraq*, and *Dirty Oil*. On YouTube, he has posted over three hundred of his own videos. With his videos, he tries to say, "You are not alone with your feelings of being overwhelmed in a culture of destruction." And, "We are all part of a whole and we can only heal when we heal everything."

Adam is respected locally and many people have encouraged him to run for elected office. He laughed and told me, "Politicians will be the last to change. Grassroots action is where the change will occur."

Grassroots is where he wants to act. He said, "What makes me work the hardest is fear for my daughters. I'll do whatever I need to do to keep them safe. If necessary, I'll teach them to Dumpster dive." He said that his life is good, with a wonderful family, good friends and work, and lots of joy. But, he said, "I had to learn how to turn my fear into courage."

He ended our conversation that day by saying, "What we have left to rescue us is our human community. That is what we have always had and, if managed properly, it will be enough."

SEVEN

All Hands on Deck

Appoint Yourself

*Does the individual know that he is the
makeweight that tips the scales?*

CARL JUNG

*God calls you to the place where your deep
gladness and the world's deep hunger meet.*

FREDERICK BUECHNER

Healthy people build healthy communities, which create
healthy cultures. And wholesome cultures foster connected communities, which produce resilient people. Change
is a spiraling process, but it can begin with each one of us.
When we act individually, we set in motion a turning that can
be deeply healing for all of us and the planet.

All of us, no matter what our situation, have great gifts to
offer the world. We can give according to our time, resources,
interests, energy, and skills. In fact, we are most likely to act
when we do that which gives us joy. Rather than ask what the

world needs, we can benefit by asking, "What do I most want to do?" Our world needs passionate people who will work at what they love.

Begin today. We need not be perfect or heroic. If we wait for that, change will never happen. Rather, let each of us busy and flawed people appoint ourselves role models, community educators, and change agents. We'll feel better when we act.

In his book, *But Will the Planet Notice?*, Gernot Wagner looks at individual versus larger-scale actions and argues that systemic economic and political changes will be necessary to save the earth. Although I understand his point, I believe he misses what is most essential. Who is it that is in charge of systemic change?

As individuals, we have no place we can begin to work except with ourselves. And individuals are always responsible for starting the actions that change cultures. Ralph Waldo Emerson wrote, "There is properly no history, only biography." My sentiments exactly.

All of us are community educators, whether we know it or not. With our every word and action, we have the power to help or to harm the world. The simplest and smallest things can sometimes be of great import. We can be a community educator every time we pick up litter on city streets, wear a T-shirt with a hopeful message, use our Facebook to share worthy information, plant flowers in empty urban spaces, or praise someone else for doing these things.

These actions may or may not make a difference to the fate of the earth over the long journey. But without question, they will make a difference in us and our communities and the quality of our lives.

Besides, we can never know the effects of our actions. The world is churning with unintended consequences. When I walk around my town, I often meet people who tell me that a particular thing I said in a therapy session or classroom made a big difference in their life. Without exception, I have always been stunned by this. Even when they repeat what it is I said that made such a difference, I generally find it hard to believe that the particular remark they mentioned would inspire any kind of transformation. I tell this story to suggest that when we do something, no matter how small, there is always the possibility that the effects of our action are larger than we know.

My mentor as a psychologist was Dr. Jim Cole. Because his influence on my life was multitudinous and profound, I have written about him in many of my books. Dr. Cole had a tradition of organizing fall and spring canoe trips down the Niobrara for the graduate students in the psychology department. He arranged the food and canoes and we all brought our own tents and sleeping gear.

As we toured the Sandhills on land and water, Dr. Cole would talk to us about the geology, the plants, and the Niobrara. He taught us about the bird migrations through the area and the local fossil beds from the time when Nebraska was part of a great inland sea.

Over time, Dr. Cole realized that the Niobrara was at risk of losing its relatively undeveloped nature. He felt a deep need to keep this river accessible and beautiful for future generations. He helped to launch a campaign to "Save the Niobrara" by having it designated a scenic river. He wrote position papers, consulted with scientists, and testified in

both state and federal hearings on the Niobrara. The Niobrara is now an official scenic river with protected status and
public access.

Thirty years after this happened, on the afternoon that I
heard of Dr. Cole's death, I happened to be sitting beside another river, the St. Vrain Creek in Colorado. Children were
laughing and shouting as they tubed down its clear, cold, and
tumbling waters. I thought of Dr. Cole's work, which allowed
children to be canoeing that day on the much slower and more
rambling Niobrara. Dr. Cole was gone, but he had left us with
a river.

Many people are intimidated by the fact that positive
change is often discussed on a policy level or in terms of man-
ufacturing windmills, solar panels, or electric cars. We are
relieved to know that someone is working in these areas, but
most of us cannot participate in these enormous projects. Acting alone, we aren't going to be reducing the acidification of
the ocean or passing federal legislation that affects water
quality.

Our situation may not allow us to form a nonprofit that har-
vests sustainable nuts from the Amazon or builds solar ovens
for people in southern Africa. People who do these things are
wonderful change agents, but they are not necessarily the best
personal role models. Possibly a better role model for us is the
guy we sit by at work who grows tomatoes in his windowsill
and knows where to buy recycled carpets. As individuals, we
don't have to build a luxury liner. But we can build a small,
sustainable boat that becomes part of a flotilla that works for
global change. Every day we can do many things to make our-

selves feel more hopeful and happy and to be part of the solution to the world's urgent problems.

Part of the trick is breaking down complicated problems into small steps. For example, my friend Hank was horrified by the amount of waste in our landfill and so he decided to challenge himself to reduce his trash. He works hard to recycle, reuse, and compost. He likes to keep track of how many wastebaskets he has to dump each week. The smaller the number, the prouder he is.

A local doctor raises prairie-grass-fed beef and sells it at the farmers' market. On Saturday mornings, he stands in front of his booth educating others about how to make prairies economically viable. He extols the quality of his beef and says that his cows do not get sick or need antibiotics or artificial supplements. They are not crowded together and they find everything they need for good health by grazing the prairie.

Betty, who teaches at nearby Doane College, treats her students to locally grown apples and organic honey. Kitty, a hairstylist, organized a fashion show to benefit local environmental causes. My friend Twyla was at my house when I threw vegetable peelings down the disposal. She looked absolutely horrified, as if I had strangled an infant in front of her. But in her gentle way, she talked to me about composting. Soon afterward, I was happily composting my coffee grinds and food scraps.

Small actions on the part of most of us can be transformative—to ourselves and to the culture. We baby boomers remember a time when there were no litter laws or recycling opportunities. Only a few years ago, we rarely saw people carrying cloth bags to the grocery store. Individual shoppers changed the situation. Every year, in the towns I visit, I notice more bike lanes. Local farmers' markets are flourishing all over the country. These wonderful new customs are happening because many people like us acted in their communities.

Generational Change

Many adults are not yet aware that their healing process and their actions to help the planet are the same thing. But our children and grandchildren are aware of this. They understand in their bones that if they are to have healthy, happy lives, they must be engaged in good work. My Baby Boomer generation's task is to keep this planet as healthy as possible until younger people are ready to take over.

In addition to enjoying our children, we all want to protect and prepare them for the future. Currently, most parents struggle with the balance between protection and preparedness. They know their children can only cope with a reality they understand, yet they can't bear to share information with their children that they cannot even face themselves.

One of the best ways to both protect and prepare children is to encourage them to act for the common good. Children love to do this and they learn many lessons from their participation in worthy projects. This kind of preparation creates resilient children, but it also is essential for the preservation of democracy. Democracy only exists because, generation after generation, people keep growing up who truly believe in it and work to make sure it continues.

A schoolteacher named Vicki recently told me, "I see too many students whose parents have raised them to think they are especially precious." She wants her sons to feel loved, but not entitled. She is preparing them to be global citizens and activists. She tells them, "You are special to me, but you live in a world of seven billion people. You have a job to do."

Every day I hear stories of idealistic children. Yesterday's story was about Benjy and his school friends. They went to the official website for *The Lorax*, a book with an environmental message by Dr. Seuss. They discovered only ads there so they created a list of ten tips to save the environment and posted it on their school's website.

The annual Christmas bird count at Spring Creek Prairie often attracts lots of families with children. As the children tromp over the prairies in their caps and heavy coats, helping their parents identify birds, they are practically dancing with glee. Not only are they having a wonderful time outdoors with the people they love and seeing many interesting animals, but they have a strong sense that they are doing something worthwhile.

Children are also effective at influencing others. Many times in the last few years, I have witnessed children's letters and testimony touch and influence hard-boiled politicians in ways that adults cannot. Politicians are people, too, and they have children and grandchildren. An articulate and earnest child who asks only for a sustainable world can soften their hearts.

I was humbled by the testimony of Sierra Club attorney

Ken Winston's daughter at a hearing about the pipeline. She said:

"My name is Helen Winston. I am fourteen years old. I am from Omaha, Nebraska. I do not stand before you as some brainwashed hippie child. I stand before you as a free-thinking young adult and as representative of the hundreds of outraged young people who couldn't make it here today.

"I represent the future, not just of Nebraska, but of America. We don't see a future for an America that relies on Filthy Oil. We don't see a future in a country where farmers are bullied from their lands while the government just stands by and watches.

"We envision a future with windmills, solar panels and hydroelectricity. We see cars running on hydrogen and clean air in our big cities. *None* of this can happen if we use this crutch, this Atrocity, that is this pipeline. I want the rest of my life to be spent drinking clean water, breathing clean air, and living in a clean Nebraska.

"So when you make your decision I want you to consider not just your future. I want you to consider my future, the future of the hundreds that I represent and the billions upon billions who will come after you. I want to end with a quote from *Star Trek*: 'The needs of many outweigh the needs of the few.' We are many, and those who would profit from this are few."

Active and Authentic Adults

Many adults who experience the awareness-to-action cycle at some point find themselves activists. Because they are connected to the world and their own hearts, they are able to see that they have no choice but to behave differently toward the world. They express their love of the world by working to change it.

I want to tell the stories of three people who appointed themselves to work for good causes. They all succeeded at moving the world forward, one millimeter at a time, but equally importantly, they all transformed anger and despair into action and authenticity.

Susan Seacrest became what I think of as a citizen scientist; that is, someone who studies an important local issue and shares her findings with all interested community members. Susan is middle-aged now, but her activism began almost thirty years ago after her toddler was diagnosed with non-Hodgkin's lymphoma. She and her husband spent a year with him on the pediatric cancer unit at the university medical center.

Shortly after her son recovered, Susan read a short article in the newspaper that said that people who lived in the Platte River Valley had a high incidence of non-Hodgkin's lymphoma. This alarmed Susan, who had always assumed that her children were growing up in a safe environment. She wrote the epidemiologist who published this study a letter asking for more information.

She had expected a form letter or a copy of the study, but instead, she received a five-page letter from the scientist. He told her that he lived far from the Great Plains and could not find the money or resources to continue his preliminary study of the Platte River. He asked Susan to do research for him on water issues in Nebraska.

With this request, Susan began her study of groundwater— a study that has lasted to this day. By now she is one of the world's leading experts on the Ogallala Aquifer and has spent her lifetime working with scientists, medical professionals, citizens, and government officials on water issues.

In every community, we have people like Susan who could (or already have) become citizen scientists on water, air quality, lead poisoning, greenhouse gases, and all of the other complex issues that are relevant to our current climate catastrophe. By acting to protect her local community, Susan did something important for herself and averted the tragedy of passivity. After a great disappointment, she transformed her pain into something that made her life more hopeful and interesting. She created meaning from sorrow.

Mitch Paine was the youngest of our coalition members and one of the first to join us. He is also one of the best grassroots organizers I've ever known. When I met him in 2010, he was a clean-cut, fresh-faced man in his twenties who dressed in a suit and tie. I mistakenly assumed he was a conservative businessman, but in fact, he was a fierce-hearted change agent. He told me that, because he looked so young, and because we live in a conservative state, he dressed in business suits to inspire respect.

When Mitch was a sophomore in high school he attended

a lecture by Jane Goodall. Afterward, he managed to speak to her and she encouraged him to keep in touch. This personal contact changed his life. He and his friend Loren started a high school chapter of Goodall's organization Roots and Shoots.

In college, Mitch lobbied for a more sustainable university. His group worked to encourage the administration to sign a pledge to try to lower greenhouse gas emissions on campus. He and the students were miles ahead of the administrators on environmental issues. In spite of a lack of any encouragement from college officials, he worked on this project all through college. Even though he was not able to make it happen, Mitch never stopped trying.

During college Mitch met Chris Beutler, Lincoln's mayor, at a conference called "Ten Points of Environmental Sustainability." The mayor spoke for only fifteen minutes, and then he listened to the attendees for an hour and a half. Mitch respected this behavior, which was unusual for a politician. Afterward, Mitch introduced himself to the mayor and the mayor invited him to breakfast the next week. He appointed Mitch to his environmental task force. This pivotal experience taught Mitch that to participate in a democracy, you must show up, meet people, and volunteer. It doesn't work to wait to be discovered.

Mitch described himself to me as an engaged citizen who works twenty-four/seven. He said, "No matter what I am doing, I try to be helping." He has run for public office in Nebraska and lost because of his progressive orientation. He has worked on a local issue—saving our rare Salt Creek tiger beetle. Mitch didn't care for the grueling fieldwork and lab work, but he liked taking photos and he used them to communicate the beetle's plight.

Like most of the members of our coalition, Mitch was not at all certain we could avert global climate change, but he knew we could win small victories by working hard. Furthermore, he was one of the happiest, most connected, and most big-hearted people I knew.

When Mitch first realized how dire the planet's situation truly was, he could have responded the way some teenagers respond. He could have self-medicated or become a smart-aleck cynic. Instead, he took a different path, and that choice made all the difference.

Randy Thompson was the most unlikely activist of our group. He had never been politically involved and liked to spend his time playing golf, drinking coffee with his neighbors, and enjoying his family. When I met him during the fight against the Keystone XL pipeline, he was a middle-aged farmer and rancher and the former operator of an auction house, or what Nebraskans call a "sale barn." Randy was a political conservative who looked like John Wayne and dressed in jeans, western shirts, and a cowboy hat and boots. He was a compelling symbol for Nebraskans. Even though he would never call himself an environmentalist, when TransCanada threatened him with eminent domain, he was outraged.

When I first heard him speak at the January 2011 rally at the capitol, he told the crowd how he became involved in the fight to stop the pipeline. He said, "TransCanada's corporate lawyers tried to bully me. They had no respect. They treated the land my parents worked so hard to keep in the family like it was a bunch of dirt."

He said that his parents got married in high school and
didn't even tell their parents for several months. They only
saw each other at school and on Saturday night dates. After
they graduated and announced their marriage, they farmed a
small piece of land. The first seven years, they had nothing
but crop failures. This was during the Great Depression and
the Dust Bowl. Randy grew up in a house with hungry people
who struggled to keep their farm. That day he told the crowd,
"When I thought of my parents and all that they had suffered
to hold on to this land, I decided to fight."

Randy showed up whenever he could be of help, and he
talked "Nebraskan." At one event he said, "That pipeline is
gonna gut our state like you do a catfish." At another, he told
a story about his barber dropping his comb on the floor. Randy
started to pick it up and the barber said, "Hold off, Randy. I
could lose my license if I handle that comb after it has been
on the floor." Randy's punch line to this story was, "We have
twenty-six pages of rules for barbers in our state and not one
law to regulate this pipeline."

He could quickly get to the heart of matters. For example, when talking about the potential pollution of our aquifer,
he asked, "Is everything in this country for sale? Do we have
anything left that doesn't go to the highest bidder?"

Randy had moved beyond, and helped others move beyond,
ideology and politics. He wasn't a polarizing figure. In fact, his
gift to our coalition was his ability to speak to every kind of
Nebraskan. Like Big Red football in Nebraska, he was able to
attract progressives and conservatives, urban and rural citizens, and university academics and farmers. At one event he
said, "All my friends warned me about radicals. But I have not

met any yet. I just keep meeting more people like me who want to protect our water and our way of life." Of the rivers and lakes in our state, he said, "There is not red water or blue water, there is only clean water or dirty water."

Despair is what inspired Randy to act. When he was bullied by TransCanada, he could have backed down and become one of those pissed-off farmers who sit around in small-town bars and talk about how the world has gone to hell. But he decided to take responsibility for saving what he loved the most.

EIGHT

The Whoosh Factor

The Wisdom of Groups

*To a small band of sowers
is given a handful of seed.*

SUFI SAYING

The transition from "me" to "we" is deeply healing to ourselves and our surroundings. Americans have always looked for great wisdom in individual heroes, and we've been disappointed when those heroes are all too human. But wisdom is not an individual characteristic; rather, it emerges from conversations between people about what is most important in their lives. In this sense, whenever we join with others to approach our situation honestly, we begin to create wisdom for our community.

Nebraskan Leo Kovar invented the phrase "the whoosh factor" to describe the momentum and creativity that his writing group inspired in its members. "Whoosh" suggests that when people come together, they can accomplish more than they can by individual actions. With this transformation from "me" to "we," the wind picks up, the sails fill, and the boat is off.

Of course, not all groups are productive and some people prefer to work alone. That being said, small groups are the Miracle-Gro—rather, the TerraCycle—for social change. Our culture doesn't often teach us that. Media coverage tends to focus on one person and doesn't point out that the heroine of a story has the support of a small group behind her. For example, Randy Thompson was the figurehead for our coalition, and as such, he became a local hero. While Randy deserved every bucket of praise he received, his success was only possible because a hundred people were working to supply him with information, plan events, and organize opportunities for him to speak on our behalf.

The modern human rights movement began with a small group of people in England in 1787. Adam Hochschild tells the story in *Bury the Chains: Prophets and Rebels in the Fight to Free an Empire's Slaves*. Twelve men came together in a London printing shop and decided to work to abolish slavery. The men developed a variety of techniques, such as consumer boycotts, education forums, posters, lapel pins, and celebrity endorsements, that are still utilized by groups today. By 1833, they had succeeded in abolishing slavery in the British Empire.

On the surface, the Rosa Parks story appears to be about one heroic woman. But in fact, Parks was part of a small group. At the time of the Montgomery Bus Boycott in 1955, she was secretary of her local NAACP, which had recently trained at the Highlander Folk School in Tennessee. Her group had discussed taking advantage of just the kind of opportunity that Parks seized. Certainly she deserves honor for her brave actions, but she did so knowing she had the support of a committed and close-knit group. When we ignore the support and grassroots training behind such a triumph, we lose an important lesson.

Grassroots groups can foster mass movements, and mass movements can lead to paradigm shifts, which can create systemic changes. If many of us are acting together now, we may have just enough time to transform ourselves into a sustainable world culture. By tackling our local issues and joining with others all over the world to work on protecting the earth, seemingly insurmountable problems may be solvable. The necessary conditions for revival are not economic ones, but rather mindfulness and community.

Still, few Americans volunteer to join groups. None of us like fractious and dull groups or ones that waste our time. However, if we are working with friends, having fun, and accomplishing something, most of us enjoy groups. The answer to the question, "Do I want to form or join a group?" generally is "It depends." It depends on our situation and it depends on the group.

Recently I met a kind woman named Charlotte, who told me, "I do my best to be helpful, but I feel silly being the only one I know who doesn't eat shrimp when the restaurants and grocery stores are filled with it. It makes me feel bitter and hopeless."

I said I knew what she meant and she continued, "If I could see our whole community responding, I would feel hope. Acting alone I just feel like a chump, but by not acting,

I feel as if I am betraying our planet." I was happy I could invite her to join the fight against the pipeline, and Charlotte jumped on board.

Facing reality need not be an excuse to feel powerless, but rather it can be a call to engagement with like-minded people. Long ago union leader Joe Hill said just before he was executed on false charges, "Don't mourn, organize."

Even in the most dire of circumstances, group actions bolster morale. When he was locked up on Robben Island, Nelson Mandela had a slogan: "Each One, Teach One." As each of the prisoners taught the others anything he knew that they didn't, the collective intelligence of the group improved.

Collective Wisdom

Margaret Mead wrote, "The ideal culture is one that finds a place for every human gift." I would paraphrase her and say the ideal group finds a place for every member's gifts. Every one of us coalition members brought our long histories, our unique skill sets, our temperaments for good or ill, and our points of view on the universe. Sometimes when members joined the group, it was hard to know how they could be helpful. But over time, everyone—no matter their limitations—was able to assist in moving our agenda forward.

Our coalition worked with whoever showed up. Few of us were even exemplars of much of anything. All of us were overcommitted. We tried to make sure that no one felt overwhelmed and that members could take time off when they needed it. But we discovered that with group support, ordinary people would do extraordinary things.

Ken is a good example of this. As an attorney, he had a full-time job as a lobbyist. He was a devoted father, a member of his church choir, and active in many other environmental groups. Often he would show up late and leave early, with our potluck meal his only meal of the day. As our pipeline work intensified, I swear, Ken grew skinnier and skinnier. One time I asked him if he ever had any free time with the woman he had been dating since his divorce. He laughed and said, "A date with my girlfriend means I answer my e-mail on her couch."

When we met for our potlucks and picnics, we practiced creative awareness; we kept up with the facts of the situation, but we didn't focus on dismal news. We looked for ways to turn challenges into opportunities for growth and action. We shared every victory and toasted every success.

Our main goal was keeping the issues around the pipeline in front of the public. We created a speakers' bureau that would talk about what we called the "Xtra Leaky." We hit the county fairs and farmers' markets. Sometimes our "crowds" were three people, but these small group meetings often turned out to be as significant as much larger ones. Often the people who came were motivated to help us with money, artwork, photos, videos, new technologies, or even legal advice.

Once at a farmers' market, a man came up and told me about his county's fight to keep the area free of hog confinement operations. Twenty years ago, they had won their lawsuit against a hog confinement owner because of an arcane state law that said no business operations could interfere with pure groundwater. Then he handed me the phone number of the lawyer who successfully argued that case. As a result, Ken called that lawyer and was able to obtain information that was later of use in a brief submitted to the legislature on behalf of groups opposing the pipeline.

As our group learned to discuss weighty matters with each other and still be calm and hopeful, we developed ideas for how to approach other people. In fact, our most common topic was communication. We quickly realized that what we knew was only useful if we could say it in ways that encouraged other people to listen and act. All of us contributed many thoughts and ideas about effective communication, but the wisdom about this was an emergent phenomenon.

We learned to use nonpolarizing language appropriate for the audiences we spoke to. Both experience and research showed us that if we wanted people to accept new evidence, we needed to present it to them in a context that didn't trigger emotional responses.

We mostly talked about what we were for, not what we were against. With almost everyone, we could find common ground and stay there. Who doesn't like clean water, green pastures, and healthy animals? We shared a deep need for a sustainable planet and for a future for our children and other people's children. Often the easiest common ground to reach was geographical: "We all love this state."

When we spoke to groups, we led with the basic premise that we were all good people doing our best, as we understood our best to be. Once that point was established, we could move into a sharing of diverse points of view.

We found messengers who could speak in the common tongue. In Nebraska the lingua franca was calmness and politeness. Nebraskans are low-key people, not fond of drama or agitation. We stayed clear of flamboyant or argumentative extremists under the theory that with friends like them, who needed enemies?

For any message in any context, we tried to find the most appropriate messenger. Nancy, Shelly, and Marge were soft-spoken, intelligent, and gifted at working with ordinary Nebraskans. Christy best represented our cause with Lincoln's progressive community. Adam, Brad, and Malinda were ideal messengers for young adults. Jane and Ben worked effectively in rural communities.

When our speakers found themselves in situations where participants had widely different opinions, we tried to utilize the word "complex." For example, when one rancher said he was not an environmentalist but only interested in protecting *his* land, our speaker said, "Exactly! But it's more complex than that. In order to protect your land, you need to work with environmentalists who have knowledge and skills that can be of use to you."

The word "complex" allowed us to include and respect all points of view. It helped those we talked to think in more reflective ways. "Complex" also gave us an opportunity with those who liked either/or questions, which were almost always false choices that pushed toward extreme answers. We could reframe those questions into more nuanced ones.

Many people distrust long-winded speakers or activists who make involved pitches for their cause. So we kept most conversations short. We developed a sense for when to stop talking or change the subject. We tried to stop at a positive point—just after we had laughed, had a moment of deep connection, or said something nurturing or hopeful. This kind of closure made it much more likely we could speak to the group again.

The summer of 2011, during the height of the pipeline furor, I attended a wedding reception in an old barn near Lincoln. It was a lovely setting with close friends, good food, and good music. Yet our coalition's work came up in almost every conversation. We'd be talking about the wedding or the beautiful summer evening, then a friend would ask me, "What is happening now with the pipeline?" I'd briefly update the person and suggest one thing that he or she might do to help our cause. Then, rapidly, one of us would turn the conversation back to the party.

Our coalition learned to always pair information with an action suggestion. People seemed to be able to afford to listen when the conversation ended with this action idea. We tailored suggestions to our listeners. Some people were willing to rearrange their lives to fight for a cause. Others, for many good reasons, were only able to do small actions.

We tried to keep suggestions doable. If we wanted four hundred people at a rally, we'd suggest that everyone try to bring a carful of people. No one person can be expected to muster four hundred people for an event, but a hundred people can each be responsible for bringing three or four people.

We tried to stay clear and current with our facts. Our coalition members read up on the issues, listened to speakers, and talked to people who really understood water, pipelines, and the politics of the issues. We fact-checked what TransCanada advertised on television or on its big billboards around the state and often we were able to dispute their inflated promises about jobs or unrealistic assurances about safety.

We grounded our coalition work in science, which often gave us a real edge when we debated opponents or talked to citizens about our position. We could refute misinformation easily. John Maynard Keynes once asked a person he was debating, "When the facts change, I change my mind. What do you do?" It turns out that many people are able to change their minds when they are presented with accurate information.

On the other hand, we learned not to expend much energy converting the converted. When we assessed our early meetings, we realized that people were there because they wanted to work and to make plans. They didn't need more evidence about problems. They wanted assignments.

We also learned not to waste our time and energy talking to people who were intractable. That never accomplished anything except to leave us feeling angry, appalled, and hopeless. Rather, we focused on people who might agree if we talked to them. To assess if a conversation with a skeptic was even possible, I would ask, "Rather than trading barbs, would you be willing to sit down with me and make a serious effort to understand each other?" If the person said no, I would move on. If the person said yes, I would say, "Great. Let's both keep our minds open and really listen to what the other says."

Coalition members learned to make our points via stories. It is impossible to argue with a story that simply reflects the experience of the storyteller. People like stories and remember them. They create emotions that are essential to motivation and action. Emotions, not facts, are what energize humans to act.

Our best stories were about our own inconsistencies and failings or about our own emotional struggles with the issue. I usually played those stories for laughs. I'd joke that in spite of my commitment to a low carbon footprint, I, like almost every other Nebraskan, want to fly to a beach in February. And I'd note that although I carry a card from the Monterey Bay Aquarium that lists which fish can be responsibly eaten anytime, my favorite fish are all on the "never eat" list—while tilapia, even with a fancy sauce on it (always a sustainable choice), tastes to me like cardboard. Most people could relate to admissions of humanity. Self-disclosure invited self-disclosure and, before we knew it, we were in an authentic conversation.

I had plenty of heartening and productive conversations. But in July 2011, I led a discussion right off the plank into the deep blue sea.

I met with a small group of people at a human services agency and explained what we were doing to stop the pipeline. I opened with brief explanations about the Xtra Leaky pipeline and the work of our coalition. The first comments came from a woman who suggested the situation was hopeless, that the good guys always lost, and that we were powerless to fight back. It went downhill from there. Other people piled on with "ain't it awful" stories and predictions of failure for us and anyone else who tried to stop big government or corporations.

I did manage to salvage a little positive energy at the end by inviting the group to act by writing letters and participating in our events. But I left wondering if the discussion had made people even more discouraged. I certainly felt worse.

Let me be clear: sharing grief and despair wasn't the problem. We all feel those things. In fact, this book is an argument that we should voice our dark emotions. However, our discussions can't stop there. Healthy conversations move through despair into something bigger and brighter. By the end of any conversation, we want to have an emotional uptick and an action plan.

As our collective wisdom grew, we were able to influence the world around us and to interact with more people who could pass their wisdom on to us. This experience of sharing our individual droplets of knowledge with others, and watching them become a beautiful wave, reminds me of a story my mother told me long ago about a hobo camp where all the men were hungry.

At first glance, it looked as if nobody had any food to share. But a wise old hobo put on a pot of water and dropped a nail in. The others were skeptical, but soon one man said, "Well, I have an onion, let's toss it in." Then another pulled out some wild carrots he'd found along the road, and another dug in his pocket for a few potatoes. As the evening wore on the soup grew richer and more savory. And finally the men had a feast, a meal that only happened because they all pitched in.

Group work is often a nail soup story. When we join with others, we create a rich stew that feeds us all a tasty meal. Any group can come together for a common cause and combine the diverse gifts and divergent points of view of its members to create something transcendent. People in groups build their own power to energize, educate, and save their communities.

Wisdom resides in people talking things over together and making decisions based on the good of all. This has been true since we sat around campfires and discussed where to hunt or look for berries the next day, and it is true now.

NINE

The Changing Tides

Our Coalition, June 2011–Aug. 2011

*It took me a long time to learn that being
miserable does not alleviate the world's
misery.*

HANNAH TENNANT-MOORE

O ur coalition felt exhilarated by the turnout and the exercise of participatory democracy by many of our citizens at the forum at the capitol in May 2011. But our sense of victory was short-lived. In fact, the situation was quite dismal.

Our Unicameral had adjourned until January 2012, and neither our attorney general nor our governor was inclined to protect our state by initiating any actions. TransCanada had many lobbyists and attorneys working with our state government to make sure that the proposed pipeline would be free of any kind of government regulation. Members of our coalition were reading in various reports and newspaper articles that the U.S. State Department was likely to approve the XL pipeline in early September. It had the power to approve the permit because the pipeline crossed the international border with Canada.

We could have despaired at this point, but to my surprise we did not. Failure and setbacks were like waves rising and falling. All of us had been aboard this boat for a long time, and we'd had plenty of experiences with storms.

From our work together we'd learned to see apparently hopeless causes as a spur to action and connection. We realized that our fight was not just about outcome, but also about our need to be engaged citizens doing the best that we could.

Besides, we were enjoying each other's company and having fun. There is a joke about a Nebraska man who is so taciturn that his wife said of him, "He loved me so much he almost told me." The men in our group were not repressed or tight-lipped this way at all, but rather, warm-hearted and articulate party starters—as were the women. As we coped with the frequent upsetting news items of the summer, we were able to nurture and support each other and leave our meetings feeling less alone and powerless.

And there were many hopeful and gratifying things to be positive about. We had created an action network across the state, which generated a great deal of support—not only in Nebraska, but all over the world. We had a process of sharing information that seemed to be working. And in spite of Trans-Canada's multimillion-dollar ad campaign, opposition to the pipeline was building everywhere.

We made sure we did work we felt like doing. If no one thought a project looked interesting, we let it go. One night I suggested that we investigate the national Chamber of Commerce's connections to fossil fuel corporations. Everyone was completely silent. Then Carol said, "I'd rather have a root canal than organize that project." I didn't want to do it myself so I dropped it.

Many people offered us their talents, their money, or their time. I learned to have a ready answer when people asked, "What can I do?" Sometimes, especially if I knew the person, I asked for help with a specific project. Other times I would say, "Here is what we are doing right now. What interests you?" Or I just would ask, "What would you most enjoy doing to help us?"

Often people would inquire if anyone had done a particular project or task. I would reply, "Great idea. How about doing it yourself? We'll help you." Often the person would look a little stunned by my response, but they would agree. Many people became active because someone in our group listened to their idea and said, "That's great. Go for it."

Well-meaning people would ask, "Have you talked to Ted Turner?" (Or it might be Arlo Guthrie or Warren Buffett or Green Day.) I would respond, "No, I am talking to you." One woman looked shocked and said, "You mean I could host an event?" I cheered her on. "Of course you can. Do you have chairs at your house and do you have any friends or neighbors? That is all you need to get started."

That summer, when things looked so hopeless, we did everything we could to "massify"—my word for building momentum and strength—and keep the issues before the Nebraska public. But by late July 2011, our coalition found itself in a strange position. Our campaigns had garnered widespread public support and crowds protesting the XL just kept getting bigger, but we hadn't been able to change laws or policies. In terms of political change, the situation was actually just as grim as it had been six months earlier. As I mentioned, our legislature was in recess, with no real protection for Nebraska in place. On the federal level, as unfathomable as it seemed, Secretary of State Hillary Clinton was expected to issue a pro-pipeline judgment in September. We were almost out of time. Unless we planned something dramatic, we were unlikely to halt the State Department's approval of the pipeline.

The Festival

At our July potluck, over sweet corn, tomatoes, and raspberry muffins, we discussed ideas for a major event. I suggested poetry readings across the state. I could ask for help from writer friends and organize it via e-mail. Ken asked, "Why restrict it to poetry? What about music and art?"

Soon everyone was tossing out ideas. We energized each other and grew more and more creative in our planning. Finally we hit upon the concept of a big festival. It would not be difficult to set up. All we had to do was set the rigging by announcing a date and having a page at Bold Nebraska's website where all events could be posted.

Randy Thompson agreed to help us promote the events and Jane suggested we call our campaign "I Stand with Randy." Bold Nebraska purchased life-size cutouts of Randy for major events and for public places. (He says the artist shaved off a few pounds to make him prettier.) In the cutouts, Randy was saying, "We will not be bullied."

Once our coalition announced the festival, our ideas whooshed. Various people planned events in their cities and small towns. These events were posted on the Bold Nebraska website and included read-ins in bookstores, storytelling and letter writing at cafés and churches, movie screenings, and an outdoor festival in Omaha featuring "Bands Against the Tar Sands." One of my favorite activities was "Grandmothers and Grandchildren Against the Pipeline." At this event, they planned to bake cookies shaped like Nebraska with chopped walnuts covering the Sandhills.

The week before the festival we launched a Burma-Shave–style slogan contest. Decades ago in rural areas, Burma-Shave, a brand of shaving cream, had been famous for its advertising gimmick of posting several sequential signs along highways. Each sign would have a few lines of a catchy verse that advertised Burma-Shave. Here are a few of the best slogans we came up with:

My husband Jim wrote, "Pipeline spill / Stop and think! / What'll you do / When you need a drink?" And, "Tar sands oil / Thick and gooey / Pipeline promises / A bunch of hooey." Neil Harrison composed, "You'll wonder / where the water went / when you are brushing / with the tar-sands excrement." Poet Marge Saiser penned, "Pipeline spill / we don't need it / Randy's warning / we will heed it."

These were hokey, but they got a lot of laughs and people in coffeehouses and city cafés all across the state had fun composing them.

Many songwriters wrote new music to old folk songs. Songs

that were easily adapted to our cause included "Which Side
Are You On?" "For the Climes They Are a-Changin'" and John
Prine's "Paradise." Below is Jim's adaptation of "This Land Is
Your Land." He has been singing his version of the song all
over the state, whenever his bands play.

> *I went out walking in the beautiful Sandhills*
> *And the stars above me shone like diamonds*
> *And the waters flowed like a river from heaven*
> *This land is made for you and me*
> *Out of nowhere comes a big old company*
> *They wanna build a pipeline where it don't belong*
> *That dirty oil ain't good for drinking*
> *This thing ain't nothing but wrong*
> *Let's walk together and raise our voices*
> *It's time to stand up to old Mr. Money*
> *They wanna buy our home, make it good for nothing*
> *But this land is made for you and me*

The weekend of the festival I immersed myself in events.
Friday afternoon I stopped and visited the art exhibit at Meadowlark. The walls were covered with dramatic paintings donated by young people. All the paintings either protested Big
Oil and the pipeline or portrayed the beauty in our state that
was at stake. The one that stood out for me was of the landscape as a woman's body. Sand cranes flew over her and a pipe
leaked oil onto her vulnerable skin.

Then I proceeded to the capitol for the "Wildflower Drop."
It was quite a scene. The halls were filled with middle-aged
women carrying Mason jars of echinacea, black-eyed Susans,

and sunflowers. On a Friday afternoon in August, the legislators and the governor were not around, but our group chatted
with their staffers, who were happy to welcome smiling visitors
with bouquets. We attached notes to our flowers that said
things such as "Please do not add oil" or "Cannot be grown in
oil." As we left the capitol, our joke was that we gave our politicians something to sneeze at!

That evening I stopped by the Forsberg Gallery to see photos of the Sandhills. I felt a lump in my throat as I looked at
the pictures of Canada geese eating grain in the fields, the
silvery Niobrara at dusk, and the old windmills, our Nebraskan mandalas. Something expanded in my heart, and I remembered what it was I was fighting for.

That evening a Nigerian artist and I cohosted "Painters
Stand with Randy" at the Burkholder Project, a boutique art
gallery in Lincoln's historic Haymarket District. The gallery
was mobbed and everyone wanted to talk.

The excitement at this event built into an oceanic swell of
energy. As we talked about saving our state, many people were
not their ordinary selves. They seemed younger, happier, and
more relaxed. I know this sounds nutty, but people actually
looked taller.

After the art gallery event, about fifty of us walked the five
blocks to the capitol. It had been raining, but at dusk the rain
stopped and a rainbow curved over the city. The air smelled
fresh and clean, and the downtown streets were buzzing with
the regular Saturday night crowds. As we walked, people
asked what we were doing, and many more of them joined us
on the spot.

A thousand other people were waiting at the capitol for

the rally to "shine a light" on Governor Heineman. The usual suspects—Jane, Randy, and I—spoke. Dressed in cowboy boots, hat, and spurs, Ben ignited the crowd when he said, "The land is not a gift from our parents. It is a loan to our grandchildren."

After the speakers, a tsunami of citizens moved across the street and painted the governor's house with light from our flashlights. Families had brought blankets, snacks, and sippy cups for the toddlers. Young people were carrying guitars and leading sing-alongs with the people around them. Some people painted pictures on the mansion's walls with the light from their flashlights, while a few held their flashlights steady in a single, accusing beam. We were a peaceful, lively crowd, but the governor didn't come out to meet us. I wondered, "What is he so afraid of?"

One woman from Hastings told the *Lincoln Journal Star*, "I don't consider myself a protestor. I consider myself a conscientious citizen trying to do what's important."

Afterward, the families headed home with their sleepy kids, while other citizens walked together to a local bar that was offering free drinks to all who were at the rally. Driving home I felt exulted, but exhausted, and this was just day one of three. As I lay in bed, memories of the day flashed before me. I swear I fell asleep smiling.

Saturday afternoon, Jim and I hosted "Poets Stand with Randy" at the Crescent Moon. When I introduced Randy in rather glowing terms, he said, "I am no hero. I am just a pissed-off farmer. I don't like bullies or being bullied."

Twyla Hansen started the reading with some prose poetry by Loren Eiseley. Then other poets read poems about water or the Sandhills region. After one poet read a poem about the Platte, the people in the room spontaneously began naming the rivers of our state. Their names—the Loup, the Niobrara, the Dismal, the Missouri, the Blue, and the Snake— were whispered as if we were praying, and they became a group poem. Randy told me he had never been to a poetry reading before. He listened intently and afterward said, "I liked this a lot more than I expected I would."

Sunday was a day filled with activity, beginning with coalition member Pippa White's adaptation of Ibsen's *The Enemy of the People*. Later in the afternoon, Mohamed, a Nebraska refugee from Sierra Leone, hosted an event in Antelope Park called "Africans Stand with Randy." It was a hot summer afternoon, but many of the guests wore colorful dashikis, caftans, and head wraps. My grandson Coltrane was with me and he was spellbound by the Sudanese music and the dancing.

Refugees from many countries in Africa attended this event, but I want to mention the Ogoni people from Nigeria whom I first met when I wrote *The Middle of Everywhere* in 2000. At that time, they had just arrived in Lincoln traumatized by what had happened in Nigeria when they tried to protest the Royal Dutch Shell oil company. Many of the men in this tribe were executed for their activism. The rest of the people had fled to refugee camps to avoid being murdered.

At Mohamed's event, the Ogoni warned us about pipelines. Their leaders stood at the mike with the park in the background and told us about their efforts to keep a pipeline from coming through their tribal lands and polluting their rivers. One of the men said, "After the pipeline came, the fish died, then the animals died, then the plants and the people died."

All of the refugees wanted to support Nebraskans' efforts to protect our state. With good reason, they were frightened of the big oil companies. In fact, Royal Dutch Shell, which plundered Nigeria, was a stakeholder in the tar sands development. Many adults stood to say that they were grateful that Randy was representing them.

Randy sat on a picnic table with his grown son and watched every speaker. He had not met refugees before, and he seemed entranced by their stories and music. When he spoke, he promised to do all he could to protect us from TransCanada. Then all of the Africans shouted, "I stand with Randy" in their tribal dialects.

The Ogoni men lined up to shake Randy's hand and be photographed with him. The whole event was extraordinary. Who would ever have imagined we would see a conservative Nebraska farmer working in solidarity with African refugees?

The grand finale on Sunday night was a dance and celebration at the Zoo Bar. We all showed up in our blue "I Stand with Randy" T-shirts. We were elated by the spiral of fun and grassroots energy that we had sparked.

The place was packed and thrumming with good cheer. The musician on stage had a sign on his guitar that read, "This guitar stops pipelines." We sang Woody Guthrie and Pete Seeger songs, then we danced to more contemporary music. The Zoo Bar manager served free drinks to members of the coalition. Senator Ken Haar, our true friend from the legislature, and Randy both spoke from the stage to wild applause and cheers. Then Ken from the Sierra Club made a toast: "This weekend was just stunning. We festivarians had experiences people rarely have in our country. It's great to be part of shining a light in the midst of darkness. Let's continue to illuminate and to communicate."

We danced, hugged, and high-fived our way through the night. We were all tired, but it didn't matter. We were connected to an energy source larger than ourselves. Everyone at the party seemed to glow from within. We had participated in something wondrous and we knew it. We felt as if we were part of the birthing of a new world.

Ken and I danced together and I noted he had been the first person to hit the dance floor that night. Ken replied, "I like to be the first person on the dance floor. I have learned that once I start dancing, everyone starts dancing." He quoted a line from a song: "You are the music while the music lasts." That is how we all felt that night. We were the music.

The Morning After

That night, we had crested a wave. But Monday morning we were in exactly the same situation with our politicians that we had been in before the festival. This bittersweet phenomenon of a successful event paired with no discernible political gain seemed to be a chronic problem for our group.

However, we were experiencing a victory that could not be taken away from us. That is, we were by now a transcendent, connected community. We were learning that relationships always trump agendas, and that a good process is sustaining, regardless of outcome. I cannot overemphasize how important relationships were to us at this point.

In fact, what I came to realize from my work with the coalition is that in individuals, families, communities, cultures, and even on earth itself, nothing good and beautiful lasts unless it is grounded in loving, interconnected relationships.

THE
TRANSCENDENT
RESPONSE

TEN

The Vast Sea Around Us

Interconnection, Deep Time, and Bliss

*Our task must be to free ourselves from
this prison by widening our circle of
compassion to embrace all living creatures
and the whole of nature in its beauty.*

ALBERT EINSTEIN

Our species is consuming, contaminating, or destroying almost everything: rivers, oceans, topsoil, prairies, fisheries, and forests, not to mention cultures. We are not behaving this way because we are cruel but rather because we are caught up in the Great Acceleration and having a hard time slowing ourselves down and thinking things through. We are living in fragmented ways, disconnected from not only each other and the natural world, but from our pasts and our futures.

Our interconnected problems are, at their roots, relationship problems. At core, every relationship has the potential to be profoundly emotional. For example, some people have a deeply emotional relationship with a particular brand of scotch. Others have this kind of relationship with their personal library. Most of us have intense relationships with our pets.

When we speak of relationships, we are talking about attachment. With attachment comes its opposite: disconnection. And with connection and disconnection come the possibility of love, anger, fear, joy, and yearning. So our real questions as humans are: what is it we are attached to, why have we selected the attachments we have, and how intensely are we attached to particular relationships? Sorting this out is a lifelong, personal challenge—and for our planet to survive intact, we must make answering these questions a global challenge, too.

We have a disordered relationship with the web of life. Healing will involve reweaving the most primal of connections to this sacred web. Interconnection can be seen as a spiritual belief, as in Buddhism, but also as a scientific fact.

As Jeremy Rifkin writes in *The Empathic Civilization*, "We are learning that the earth functions like an invisible organism. We are the various cells of one living being. Those who work to save the earth are its antibodies."

Whether we like it or not, we are all in this together. As Gregory Bateson reminds us, the unit of survival is the individual and her environment. Enlightened self-interest should make environmentalists of us all. When we destroy an old-growth forest, we lose many plant and animal species that could be of great use to humans in fighting diseases. If the rain forests go, the planet loses its lungs and we all will die. When the insects disappear, how do we plan to survive? We humans don't know how to pollinate fruit.

The distinction that English makes between humans and their environment—an "us" versus "it" distinction—encourages a disordered relationship to the earth. A sense of separation is implied by the word "nature." People often speak as if they were not a part of nature, as if nature were rather something to control, use, or enjoy. We cannot fix the earth the way we fix a car or a dishwasher. We are a vital part of the organic whole. Thich Nhat Hanh talks about dualism this way: "We need to move beyond the idea of 'environment' and fall back in love with Mother Earth."

Moral Imagination

If we do not expand our vehicles of mercy and ways of helping each other, we will destroy ourselves. To adaptively cope with our global storm, we need to enlarge our moral imaginations in order to include all living beings in our circle of caring.

At its most basic, the moral imagination is respect for point of view. It is similar to empathy, but more complex. Neuroscientist Antonio Damasio has done research that distinguishes between the two processes. In the brain, empathy can be a simple and often short-term process that involves mirror neurons. For example, we might feel an instant identification with a person who falls down or a kitten who hisses when it is afraid. Neurologically, our response to other people's situations can also be a more whole-brained response that is slow to develop and longer lasting. I am calling this response "moral imagination."

My understanding of the moral imagination allows me to have a clear and simple value system. Good is that which increases my own and/or the collective moral imagination. Evil is that which decreases these things. I believe that the purpose of life is to grow our moral imaginations and to help others grow theirs.

With a well-developed moral imagination, there is no "us" and no "them." We are all us. This concept is similar to Martin Buber's distinction between I-It and I-Thou relationships. The moral imagination allows us to make every relationship we are in—with our families and friends, with our coworkers and the clerks at the stores, and with the animals and plants around us—a sacred relationship.

Reconnection with All Living Beings

All of my life, I have been devoted to animals. I have never been able to see them as merely resources for humans to utilize. By the time I was eight, I ran my own animal rescue program. After summer storms, I would walk through the streets of my hometown searching under trees and in gutters for baby animals who needed my protection. I would bring home mice, squirrels, or birds and nurse them with a rag dipped in milk. I'd construct little homes for them from shoe boxes and, every now and then, I would actually save an animal and release her into the wild.

Most children are gradually educated away from this deep connection to animals. But I resisted that indoctrination. As a child, I named every little starling or field mouse I rescued as well as all the calves, pigs, and rabbits that my father raised for food. This caused me all sorts of problems. I cried when I buried my unsuccessfully "rescued" animals and I said long, tearful good-byes before my dad butchered animals that he considered livestock. That irritated him to no end.

My folks had grown up during the Depression and they couldn't afford much empathy toward farm animals. They weren't picky eaters. My dad knew how to cook everything from squirrels to snakes, turtles, and possums. We children ate what was before us or we went hungry. Usually I ate whatever was served, but afterward, I had nightmares in which the animal came to me and asked me to spare his life, or worse, the animal in question saved my life.

In high school in the late 1960s, I tangled with my biology teacher, Mr. Davidson. For our science homework he insisted we catch and euthanize butterflies and then pin them onto foam board. The more varieties we killed, the higher our grade. I didn't want to do this project and, after school, I visited Mr. Davidson's classroom to discuss it with him. I explained that I thought we could learn more by watching the butterflies in the wild than by killing them, especially the rare ones. I also confessed that I didn't like to kill anything. Mr. Davidson explained anthropomorphism to me and said sternly, "You can't be a scientist if you think that animals have feelings."

His comments didn't bother me. I didn't want to be a scientist. I wanted to befriend the animal kingdom and learn the names of all the birds, insects, and local plants.

Even today I am not fond of the word "anthropomorphic." Of course it has some utility. Worms probably don't miss their mothers and humans have a tendency to overinterpret our pets' expressions. Certainly we can't accurately understand animals by simply projecting our ideas onto them. However, the word "anthropomorphism" minimizes our deep connection and interdependency with all living beings. We do this at great peril. Only when we see the world realistically as an interconnected and continuously interacting circle of worthy beings can we respond appropriately to all levels of our global environmental crisis.

Anthropomorphism is a Western concept. All over the world indigenous people listen to and speak to animals. They know animals have personalities and spirits, just like people do. Not so long ago, all of us knew the language of animals and could speak to them.

I also ran aground with English teachers who corrected my use of the word "who" in dependent clauses that refer to animals. I know the rules—"who" is for people and "that" is for places and things—but I always write or say "who," as in, "The coyote who lived with us developed a slight limp." Or, "The possum who lives in our window box likes to forage in our compost pile." In this book, I am not correcting my lifelong grammatical idiosyncrasy. In fact, I hope some people adopt this small custom.

Many children today, because of their limited contact with animals, struggle to develop a sense of kinship with living beings. I once watched a nature educator give a talk to fourth graders. She talked about the animals of the prairie and then placed a taxidermied coyote on a table so that the children could touch its fur. A little girl with pigtails and a *Hannah Montana* T-shirt raised her hand and inquired, "Has this coyote been sanitized?" During the season of H1N1, her question was sensible. Yet I suspect it was one never before asked in the history of childhood.

We can expand children's moral imaginations by helping them understand the point of view of others. Dr. Seuss was good at this, as was Shel Silverstein. One day I played my grandchildren a song from a book called *Hey, Little Ant* by Phillip and Hannah Hoose and Deb Tilley. This song is a conversation between an ant and a boy on a playground, whose friends are watching. The boy wants to squish an ant just for fun. But the ant sings that he has a home and a family, too. He sings to show the boy that his life is as precious to his ant family as the boy's life is to his human family. The song ends with a question for the listener to ponder, "Should the ant get squished? Should the ant go free? / It's up to the kid, not up to me / We'll leave the kid with the raised-up shoe. / What do you think that kid should do?"

I asked my grandchildren what they would do if they were the boy with the raised-up shoe. When nine-year-old Kate heard it, she said, "Nonna, I'll never squish an ant again." Seven-year-old Aidan also promised to let all ants run free. But five-year-old Claire said, "Nonna, I still like to squish ants but I won't kill any talking ants." Sigh. She'll have a growth spurt soon enough.

One summer afternoon I made a deep connection with a

wild animal. I was cleaning roots and twigs from an underground electrical box when my hand connected with stiff fur. That startled me, but not nearly as much as the jolt I felt when the fur began to move under my fingertips. I pulled back my hand and peered into the darkness. I could see thick silver fur.

I guessed that it belonged to a possum. No doubt he was readying a home for the cold Nebraska winter. I wished I could have just left him alone in his newly prepared winter home, but because of the electrical circuitry, that option was too dangerous for him and for us. I didn't want to harm him, but I needed to evict him.

First I propped open the lid and banged gently on it with a hammer. Then I drummed louder. The possum, well, he played possum. I decided to leave for a while to allow him to retreat with his dignity intact.

When I returned fifteen minutes later he was still there. I banged again, to no noticeable effect, then I carefully prodded him with a broom. That got his attention. He sat up, bared his teeth, and hissed at me, but he stayed put.

I poked gently at him some more. He hissed sadly at me. I again retreated, but returned every twenty minutes to check on the situation.

In the box sat the possum, wide-awake and looking at me with mournful eyes. I peered into his red eyes and discerned he was asking me, "Really, do I have to leave? I have worked so hard to gather all these twigs and grasses. I like it here. I won't harm you, I promise."

I tried to convey, "I am sorry. I wish you could stay. I know you have as much right to this place as I do. But I don't want you to be hurt. Please leave here, but stay anyplace else you like."

When that little possum and I looked in each other's eyes, I could recognize our resplendent kinship. I didn't feel superior to him, or afraid of him, or even that much different from him. We were both hoping for a safe berth for the coming winter. We were both alive and breathing under the same Nebraska sky.

We had a moment. Actually, we had many moments all afternoon. I think I understood the possum's point of view quite well, but he never seemed to understand mine. Late that afternoon, I called Animal Control for help. But I stipulated, "Don't send anyone unless they can guarantee to free the possum without harming him."

A worker came and chatted with me about the situation. Then she gently removed him with long-handled tongs. He hissed in fear, but he wasn't hurt in any way, except perhaps his pride. The possum looked to be about fifteen months old and was unusually silvery. The worker released him immediately and he toddled over to a nearby fir tree. Since then, he has moved into one of our window wells. I've named him Blinky.

~~~~~~~~~~

When I experience these kind of moments with an animal, I realize how interwoven our lives are with the lives of all living beings. The poet Pablo Neruda wrote, "We are each one leaf on the great human tree." I would paraphrase, "We are each one leaf on the great green tree of all living beings."

We all form environments for each other. I am the possum's environment and he is mine. We are the relatives of the oak tree and the mosquito, the yucca and the fox. We "inter-are," as Thich Nhat Hanh would say. As a species we will survive only if we are able to restore our ancient and true awareness of a connected universe.

Deep Time

One of the most healing practices in terms of coping with the Great Acceleration is to connect with deep time, which I define as the time since the world began to the time when the world will end. All of us are built of time, just as a mountain or a saguaro is built of time. Often, we forget this and live on our small, eroding island of time as if it were a continent. That forgetting is inevitable, but it's also sad. When we lose our connections to deep time, we lose our sense of the vastness and wonder of life, and our perspective about our place in the grand seascape of time.

LUCA, an acronym for the last universal common ancestor, probably dates to around 3.8 million years ago. At that time, LUCA was bobbing around on ocean waves with neither worries nor neighbors. Our human ancestors differentiated from other living beings about one billion years ago. Then four hundred million years ago, the earliest froglike beings developed joints on their pectoral and pelvic fins and slithered out of the sea onto land.

About 1.8 million years ago, our African ancestors moved north into the Caucasus and slowly spread out across what is now Europe and Asia. Roughly forty thousand years ago, people crossed what we call the Bering Sea into the great landmass of the northern hemisphere. Almost one thousand years ago, Europeans built small boats and sailed across unknown oceans toward an unknown land.

Recently, when my friend Jeremy and I were weeding my garden, he asked me what I thought drove evolution. I realized as I pondered this question that even though I had a degree in anthropology, I had never seriously considered it before. Obviously I could explain the scientific facts of evolution, but Jeremy was asking me why evolution occurred. He might as well have asked what motivates God.

As I thought about how to answer, I realized that I believe the same things that motivate me motivate evolution. How human of me! My life goal is to grow in moral imagination and to develop all of my gifts so that I can utilize them for the benefit of myself and all living beings. I think the goal of all living beings is to fully realize their incipient gifts and to grow into more complete, differentiated, and integrated beings.

There is a great comfort in connecting to deep time. We can connect to it by thinking about the family members who came before us and about those who will come long after we are dust. We can connect with deep time in places like the Grand Canyon or in the great cathedrals of redwoods in the Northwest and California.

My friend Jane, who lost her husband recently, spent time on the New Jersey coast counting the waves—one hundred for all of the sorrows and then one hundred more for acceptance and peace. She told me, "The ocean has a way of putting things into perspective."

One of my favorite books is Bill McKibben's *The Age of Missing Information*. In it, he compares what he learns by locking himself into a hotel room and watching nonstop television for two days with what he learns when he climbs a mountain by himself and sits quietly for two days. The book is a wonderful exploration of the differences between what we need and what we get. One of the most profound insights McKibben had was that when he watched television, he felt dissatisfied with himself, deprived, and overstimulated. He found himself constantly wanting pizza and worrying about what kind of electronics to buy. When he sat on a mountain, he felt at peace with the world, extraordinarily grateful to be alive, and calm. He was able to connect with deep time and put his own life in the perspective of an ancient and enormous universe.

One of the wonderful benefits of realizing one's smallness in the context of an immeasurable universe is that, contrary to logic, this experience does not make most people feel powerless and insignificant. Rather, it allows us to feel safe, connected, and comforted. Whether we are on a mountaintop, a prairie, a beach, or a desert, the timelessness and vastness of what we can experience makes us feel as if we are rocking in the great creel of time.

Ironically, we can connect with deep time by truly living in the present moment. The present moment has everything that ever happened and will ever happen embedded within it. When we experience a moment of being truly awake and alive, we automatically connect with all that is truly awake and alive now.

After a family day one July, my son Zeke told me, "I had a good moment this afternoon. I was swimming with my kids and thinking about barbecue and a ball game in the evening. Everyone was getting along and having fun. Suddenly, a feeling came over me. Time stopped for a minute and the shouts of the kids faded away. I felt blissful. It was the feeling that this moment was sufficient. I needed no better moments. Everything was right in my universe." That same day, my granddaughter Kate asked my daughter, "If you knew you had only twenty-four hours left, how would you want to spend it?" Sara answered, "Just like today."

Bliss

I was quite old before I realized that the antidote to despair is not just work. The most powerful antidote to despair is bliss.

One Friday night, I was weary after a long workweek and in a wired/spaced frame of mind. As I drove out to Jim's bluegrass gig at a nearby winery, my head buzzed with the sad little details of life. When I stepped out into the dark, I was hardly aware of anything but my whirring brain. But I happened to glance up and see a half-moon caught in the branches of an ancient oak tree. That silvery moon in its cradle of branches stopped me in my tracks. I could have fallen to the ground in prayer, it was so beautiful. My breathing changed and I was intensely and perfectly present. By the time I walked into the winery to join my friends, I felt new. Bless the world's heart for giving me the chance to see beauty anywhere, whenever I open my eyes. Bless the world's heart.

Bliss and wonder are transcendent states, but there are many ways to transcend our ordinary consciousness. All of them involve being in the present moment and experiencing a connection to a world much more ancient and much larger than our little, limited selves.

In our moments of wholeness we can suddenly imbibe the heart-cracking beauty of it all.

When I met Brad Kindler, he was a twenty-nine-year-old farmer who often wore a knit cap covering his hip-length straight brown hair. He worked at a community action program teaching people how to make their homes more energy efficient and giving workshops on permaculture, rain barrels, and composting. He was someone who could inhabit a moment and spot a miracle. He excelled at orchestrating bliss.

Brad radiated authenticity, enthusiasm, and goodwill. What I most appreciated about him was the quality of attention he gave to the moment he was in. And he was the only person I knew who never seemed to be in a hurry.

One day Brad was working in my garden barefoot and shirtless, in a pair of overalls. His hair was tied in a ponytail. He called me over to where he had paused under a large Scotch pine. He told me to stand quietly and listen. When I did, I heard a sound like rustling dry leaves or popcorn popping or maybe a fire burning. It wasn't loud but it was a sound I had never heard before.

"I've been trying to figure this out and I think I've got it," Brad said. "That is the sound of sap rising in this tree." He explained we had experienced such a cold, wet spring that the sap had not risen gradually over several weeks as it usually does. Then that day, on our first sunny hot day, the sap had exploded out of the ground and into the tree. We were hearing it move up into the branches. "Crackle, crackle."

We stood for a long time listening to what was our first, and perhaps our only, experience of this amazing event. Brad had found us a miracle.

Brad's activism began with an upsetting event in high school. His senior year he was old enough to vote for the first time. He researched all the candidates—local, state, and presidential—and he wrote detailed analyses about who he would vote for and why. He was excited and honored to participate in our democracy. However, the year was 2000, with the complicated Gore/Bush postelection nightmare. To make matters worse, not one candidate whom Brad voted for was elected. That made him rethink his approach to being a citizen.

He felt discouraged because it seemed that voting was really no power at all. The only way to participate in a democracy was by active engagement. He began to join demonstrations and plan events supporting environmental causes. One of the first he organized was a bike ride to ShadowBrook Farm's Harvest Festival. He thought a few friends would show up, but forty people turned out.

Brad was a big believer in staying put. He knew that the earth could be enjoyed almost everywhere. When he talked about our state, he said, "Here in Nebraska I have seen Bishop Tutu, Gorbachev, Ani DiFranco, and Dylan."

"We can do everything possible to save the earth right

where we are, but we have to show up," Brad said. Then he laughed. "Sometimes, I am tired and not in the mood or I think, this is gonna suck, but I go. I try to pay attention, contribute, and be open to the experience. Sometimes I am amazed by what happens."

When I picture Brad, I see him landscaping for a local Buddhist temple or greeting people at the ShadowBrook booth at the farmers' market or playing banjo in the kitchen as his friends cook or dancing late at night to a Cuban band at the Zoo Bar. Somehow he has managed to be passionate and calm, aware and happy. He said, "My experiences as an activist have taught me how much fun I can have. My life is not a sacrifice but full of adventures."

As we go about our troubled and sometimes frenzied lives, in this time of the Great Acceleration, we have close at hand ways we can move out of the time zone of our current century and into a transcendent experience. We can do this by simply recognizing our kinship with another living being, by finding one beautiful thing to enjoy, or by allowing ourselves to be swept away emotionally by the miraculous and intricate world we have all around us.

ELEVEN

The Darkening Skies

Our Coalition, Sept. 2011–May 2012

*Hope is not the conviction that something
will turn out well, but the certainty that
something makes sense, regardless of how it
will turn out.*

VÁCLAV HAVEL

After our joyous August festival things happened quickly. The farmers turned to the harvest, and the university students returned to campus. However, Nebraskans were riled and did not forget that TransCanada was still at work. At our first Big Red football game of the season, eighty-five thousand fans booed when a TransCanada ad flashed on the jumbo screen in the stadium. The next day the University of Nebraska's chancellor announced that TransCanada would no longer be allowed to advertise at university events.

Bowing to popular pressure and looking toward his next election, Governor Heineman wrote a letter asking President Obama to reroute the pipeline so it wouldn't go through the

Sandhills and over the aquifer. Members of our coalition knew Heineman was playing a political game. He wrote this letter to pass the buck to President Obama. Then, when the White House supported TransCanada's decisions about a route, which he fully expected the president would do, Governor Heineman could blame Obama for not protecting us. But much to the governor's surprise, Obama responded to his letter by delaying the pipeline process and calling for more environmental reviews. In fact, the president often cited our Republican governor as his reason for denying the pipeline permit.

Around this time, many pipeline opponents flew to Washington, D.C., to protest the tar sands development alongside thousands of other Americans. Thirty of our citizens were arrested while peacefully protesting. Handsome, articulate Ben was asked to tell our state's story at the national protest. A photo of Nancy made the front page of our local newspaper. Gray-haired schoolteacher-grandmother-pie-baker Nancy was shown handcuffed in her "I Stand with Randy" T-shirt. Mohamed also was photographed in handcuffs. He looked sweet, serene, and somber. How brave he was: a Muslim man who had been imprisoned in his home country, volunteering to be arrested once more.

Almost before we could acknowledge our victories with Heineman and in Washington, D.C., the State Department held public hearings in Lincoln and the small town of Atkinson. More than a thousand Nebraskans showed up at both places to testify against the pipeline.

The Apple Pie Brigade

Around that time Nancy and I began meeting outside the governor's mansion every Monday at noon for what we called the "Thank You in Advance Campaign." At first, it was just the two of us, but soon several other grandmothers joined. We brought our governor small gifts such as cinnamon rolls, pies, or flowers and vegetables from our gardens and also letters thanking him in advance for calling a special session to debate the routing of the pipeline, something we knew he had no intention of doing.

Week after week we delivered our gifts and letters. We chatted with each other while we waited for a security guard to accept our gifts. Afterward, we walked across the street to the capitol and climbed the stairs to Governor Heineman's office. For two months we politely requested a meeting and every week our request was denied.

I suspect we will never know why, but in October the governor called a special session to discuss the routing of the pipeline. Our coalition members speculated that, once again, Heineman was trying to pass the buck—this time to the legislature, who wanted to avoid the responsibility for regulating pipelines as much as he did.

Finally, when the special session met in November 2011, our little group caught a break. As we were trying to schedule an appointment with the governor, I recognized a former neighbor who worked for him. I told him about our frustration concerning scheduling and asked him why the governor wouldn't meet with his constituents. The next day we had our meeting.

Seven of us grandmothers visited the governor. Nancy brought along her eleven-month-old granddaughter Mollie. I joked with Governor Heineman that he would like at least one member of our group and I pointed to Mollie. He laughed and that helped the meeting start gracefully. As Mollie crawled under the table, sat on various laps, and babbled happily away, she helped us stay relaxed.

The governor generously gave us an hour of his time. We listened to what he had to say, which was that he also wanted to protect our state and was working with the legislature and TransCanada to make sure that everything would be done in a safe and responsible manner.

Then we asked questions that were polite but pointed.

Nancy asked why the governor had not introduced legislation himself that would protect our state. I asked why Trans-Canada had access to politicians but citizens did not. Penny asked why something was happening in our state that the vast majority of Nebraskans opposed. After the governor used the word "environmentalist" with contempt, Marge pointed out that Nebraska's environmentalists were his constituents, while TransCanada, a foreign corporation, was not.

We asked that he commit to sign any legislation that crossed his desk that would reroute the pipeline out of the Sandhills and the aquifer area. He wouldn't agree to do this, which we felt was a strong indication that he was in the pockets of TransCanada. We ended the meeting by saying that if he protected our Sandhills the best cook in our group would bake him an apple pie. As he walked us out, he waxed eloquent about his mother's great pies.

After the meeting we agreed that we had succeeded in two ways. We had shown the governor the nonradical faces of citizens who opposed the pipeline. In fact, all of us happened to be former teachers, not by nature a profession that attracts hotheads. And we put Governor Heineman on notice that some of his citizens were very aware of what was going on and that it would not be easy to spin any stories that capitulated to TransCanada.

Action as an Antidote to Despair

Not surprisingly, most of our legislators were angry at the governor for calling the special session and tossing them the political hot potato. To be honest, this game would have been funny if we didn't have so much at stake. Most of the senators were collaborating with TransCanada. In fact, before the special session, TransCanada's attorneys briefed legislative staffs, and their lobbyists and their public relations staff partnered with the pipefitter unions, sponsored our state fair, and even sent the consul general of Canada to Lincoln to urge lawmakers to help with the pipeline.

On the other hand, ordinary citizens had no voice in the proceedings. Our coalition decided to call our own special session. We held it in the chamber across from the one in which the Unicameral was meeting. I opened the packed meeting with these remarks:

"This beautiful bounty that we have known—the land, the

water, the trees and grasses—is not just the cornerstone for how we survive, it is the very fabric of who we are. We live in Nebraska and Nebraska lives in us."

I told a story about my own grandson. "When Aidan was six, he had a growth spurt in point of view. Our family had gone to a lake to watch the Perseid meteor showers. Kate had already seen falling stars before and was interested, but not amazed, by the evening. Claire, at four, wanted to see the Perseids, but never managed to settle down and look up at the sky. But Aidan lay in the grass beside me, holding my hand. He said, 'I want to see my first falling star with you, Nonna.' When a meteor blazed across the sky and into the lake, we both inhaled and I said, 'We'll never forget this moment.'

"Afterward, driving back home, we crested a hill and Aidan saw the lights of his small town on the horizon. He said, 'Look at my beautiful city.' I responded, 'It is a pretty town at night with all the twinkling lights.' Aidan was quiet for a moment and then said, 'Nonna, my town is big to me, but small to the rest of the world.'

"I sighed and told Aidan, 'That is a lesson we all have to learn sooner or later.'"

I concluded my remarks at our special session by saying, "Aidan may be small to TransCanada. He may be small to our legislators and our governor. But he is big to me and I am going to take care of him."

Scientists, attorneys, and concerned citizens testified that day. Randy spoke last. He said, "When I think of our grandchildren's children, I think, Will they thank God our ancestors had the foresight to protect our water or will they ask, What were the damn fools thinking about?"

After our coalition's special session, our members followed with intense interest the newspaper reports of the ups and downs in the legislative process, as it concerned not only TransCanada, but all further pipeline regulation in the state. TransCanada continued to work behind the scenes for a bill that exempted it from any rules that would control pipelines in the state, on the grounds that it had a permit pending.

On the other hand, much to our surprise, another bill, LB 1, which passed, set up a reasonable and unbiased process to regulate all future pipelines. None of us were exactly sure how this useful bill came about. As I mentioned, we had little access to the negotiations. What we do know is that many senators, while supporting TransCanada's special legislation, also felt the need to forestall more pipeline drama in the future. We speculated that they wanted to be able to run in their home districts on the "right" side of an issue that was important to voters. To give many of the legislators credit, they— like the rest of us—have children and grandchildren, and no doubt hoped to protect the state for them.

In addition to the wins with the legislature, that same month, President Obama announced that he was ordering TransCanada to consider a route that didn't cut through the Sandhills.

By the end of the monthlong special session, our coalition members felt proud of ourselves. We had achieved what seemed impossible only months earlier. We had begun as a small group of people in my living room and ended up a force to be reckoned with. At our holiday party in December, we cracked open bottles of champagne and took turns toasting each other for our roles in the victories.

If the story had stopped here, the work of our coalition

would have been one of the great environmental victories of the decade. If only the story had stopped here.

Winter

In January 2012, President Obama denied a permit to Trans-Canada, the first and only international pipeline permit ever denied by the U.S. government. Originally, our group was elated by his decision. But rapidly that elation turned to moderate alarm, as we watched what was perhaps the primary environmental issue on earth become an ideological hot button.

That same month, Nebraska's legislature convened and quickly the senators began to confer with TransCanada about how to deal with the new situation. The corporation no longer had a permit, but that did not stop it from wanting special legislation. Furthermore, TransCanada needed the support of our Nebraska politicians to be able to make the argument that the president's concerns had been addressed. If TransCanada could say that Nebraskans were satisfied with the pipeline route through their state, the company could legitimately ask, "What does Obama object to now?"

On February 16, 2012, I attended the committee meeting in which Senator Jim Smith introduced a bill written to privilege TransCanada, even though it had no pipeline permit pending. The room was packed with members of our coalition, ranchers, and other concerned citizens. The committee chairman first asked Senator Smith to read his bill and explain it to the committee. Senator Smith, a short, portly man dressed in a business suit, read the bill but could not answer one single question about it. In fact, he deferred all questions to the representative from TransCanada who had flown in just for this meeting.

This representative spoke to the committee next. He was dressed in an expensive suit and shoes. He addressed the committee chairman by his first name and asked about his winter hunting season. He expressed his happiness to be back in Nebraska and his love for our state and his great respect for our senators. Then he proceeded to explain how TransCanada had only the interests of Nebraska at heart, and that this bill would do nothing but make our state more prosperous and healthy. We could trust him on this.

He was then asked a few questions by the committee about the specifics of the bill. These were not questions about the bill's reasonableness or safety, but were instead legal questions about how the state could avoid being sued for passing legislation that privileged TransCanada. The representative from TransCanada deferred these questions to the company attorney, who seemed more familiar with the bill than Senator Smith.

This lawyer then approached the committee and explained the logic of the bill. He reassured the committee that it would be legal. Following this man's testimony, one other person in this room of two hundred people spoke in favor of the bill. That was the head of Nebraska's Department of Environmental Quality and a close cohort of the TransCanada team. His testimony in favor of the bill was unprecedented. Heads of state agencies are asked to provide relevant information to committees, but they are expected to be impartial. After these four proponents of the bill finished, the room exploded with Nebraska citizens who were angry and upset about their lack of representation.

Following that day, there were no positive changes with our state government. And in fact, on April 11, 2012, with only the objections of a few brave legislators, Senator Smith's bill was passed. LB 1161 rubber-stamped an undetermined route through the state for the Keystone XL tar sands pipeline and granted TransCanada the authority to use eminent domain to forcibly take Nebraskans' land. That bill undermined any safety reviews and barred opportunities for a public review of the later route. It also gutted the public service commission process for reviewing pipelines adopted during the special session in November 2011. In fact, this bill left us in a worse situation than when we had no legislation at all.

Even more alarming, most Nebraskans were not aware of this bill and its ramifications. Everywhere coalition members went, we met people who congratulated us on our great victory. They assumed that we had won and our state was protected. We knew otherwise, and we tried to explain why and what we had lost. That wasn't much fun.

All of our efforts to protect our state, at least for the moment, appeared to have ended with the state even deeper in the pockets of TransCanada with our land and water more compromised than ever.

Hope

The night after the passage of LB 1161, our coalition had a meeting scheduled. All of us arrived at Christy's house knowing exactly what had happened. When Ken walked in he said, "I feel like I have spent my day juggling chainsaws." I opened the meeting by saying, "This is a sad day for the state of Nebraska and for everyone at this table. Does anyone want to speak further about this day's events?" No one did.

People looked discouraged for a few moments while we passed around nachos and beers. Then we began talking about our participation in Connect the Dots on Climate Change Day, May 5, 2012, an international happening sponsored by 350.org.

All of our despair about the day's events was alchemized into anticipation and hope as we planned our specific event, "Give Our Children a Future." Shelly offered to donate free Dippin' Dots, Adam said he'd bring lemonade in compostable cups from Meadowlark, and Ken—a musician himself—promised to find great musicians.

This planning occupied about an hour of our time and cheered us up immensely. I realized that, in fact, the vigor of our planning was directly related to the disappointments of the day. We needed to make something big and joyful happen in order to move on emotionally ourselves, and by channeling all of our distress we had the emotional propulsion to do it.

After dinner, I looked around the table at our group with pride. Everyone at that table had done everything they could to make the earth a better place. For the most part, while our actions succeeded on small levels, on the larger level, we had

been defeated over and over. And yet we kept going, unde-
terred. On impulse, I told the group, "I'd like to ask everyone
how they keep going and caring in the face of continual defeat."

Christy, whose son had developed AIDS from blood trans-
fusions for his hemophilia and died young, had had a life
filled with challenges. She was one of Lincoln's most active
advocates for human rights and a member of the Amnesty
International board. I had known her when she was a beautiful young violin player, teaching Spanish at Lincoln High
School. But by now, she was in her sixties and, like me, gray
haired with a face lined by the years. She began by saying, "I
have been on the margins since high school. My senior year,
our school had a mock election. Of all the students and fac-
ulty, I was the only one who voted for Adlai Stevenson." Everyone laughed because, for the most part, that type of defeat
had been a common occurrence for many of us.

Christy was thoughtful a minute and then spoke. "I do it
for the relationships. I like to spend my time with people who
are trying to make the world a fairer, kinder place. I've been
in groups like this since college, and they have made me
happy. The people who stand up to power are who I choose to
be with."

Nancy looked almost perplexed by the question and simply
said, "I am a trudger. I just don't know any other way to be. If
I believe in something, I'll keep working."

Jane said, "I fight because they expect me to give up." Her
voice had a slightly angry edge, but she was smiling in a
charming, ornery way.

Her fierceness was understandable. For years she had been
attacked mercilessly by conservative legislators for her progres-

sive stands on everything from health care to the need for more regulation of water and energy in our state. On the other hand, what was amazing about Jane was her good humor and persistence in the face of so much public criticism.

The next person to speak was one of our newest members, Wesaam. He was a young, handsome man from the Middle East. He had had many traumatic experiences in refugee camps as a child, but instead of making him bitter, they had filled him with love and an eagerness to help other people. It was clear he had thought about questions such as the one I had posed. His response was, "Too many people only dream at night. I like to dream during the day."

He continued to explain that all of his life, in difficult situations, he had coped with his own despair by trying to be useful and to cheer other people up. He said, "Hope became my identity."

Ken spoke next. His lanky frame was slumped with exhaustion. He had just lost a hard fight in the legislature, but he said defiantly, "I keep fighting because I won't let those jerks win. I'm not going to just lie down and take it. And I do it for my kids."

By now, the attention of the entire group was focused on these answers. The room was quiet, except for the speaker, and people were listening as if somehow their lives depended upon what the other people said. I realized, looking around the table, that this was the conversation we most needed to have that night. We were teaching each other lessons in resilience.

It was my turn next, and I quoted neuroscientist Dan Siegel, who said, "The mind functions best when it feels hope."

Swallowing hard, I said, "I do this work because acting as if I have hope gives me hope. The process of trying to make things better is the healthiest way I have of responding to the world around me."

Carol, the constant and generous worker bee of our group, looked sad. Her voice was flat when she said, "I have no hope." She paused and then said, "I just don't know any other way to spend my life than doing this work."

Next to Carol sat Buffalo Bruce. He was a skinny guy who had been involved in local progressive causes for a long time. He held up his shot glass, which had the word "Doomed" etched on it. He said, "See this shot glass and the bourbon in it? That's what gives me hope."

Sitting next to Buffalo Bruce was our wonderful Dippin' Dots poet, Shelly. She is a born cheerleader. She had been listening with great respect to everyone's comments, but when it was her turn to speak, she said—in her perky and deceptively innocent way—"You guys are entitled to think whatever you think. But I think we're gonna win. I think it's all gonna work out. And I think we *are* going to succeed at leaving our grandchildren a sustainable planet."

That was such a surprising idea that we all sat in shock for a moment. Finally, I laughed and said, "Shelly, we need to clone you and bring about a dozen more of you into this group."

Marian said, "I may be a little shallow, but my mood is generally happy and optimistic. I don't think too much about the big picture. I just try to do what I can every day. I feel good about the small victories that come my way. For example, recently an evangelical group from Crete, Nebraska, began coming to the prairie and learning to love it. They are now interested in working with us and with local environmentalists to protect the prairie. That was a real victory."

She sighed and frowned before she continued speaking. "When I think about my life, I think I am ridiculous. Every week I take on these enormous, unmanageable projects— projects that would exhaust and deplete a whole group of people, let alone myself. But I have a way of framing things that works for me. It comes from the time when I was a nurse. When my favorite patient died, I was grief stricken. I cried and cried. But then I realized if I were going to work in nursing, I would need sufficient detachment from my patients' deaths to be able to stay calm and cheerful. So I developed those skills. I learned to be with people I really loved and know they were dying, and sometimes see them die. That detachment has been a good thing in my work with the environment.

"My training as a nurse was good training for caring for a prairie. I feel as if the prairie is now my patient. I love this patient and want to do everything I can to keep her healthy."

Christy's husband, Dick, also a long-term activist, said, "I do all this work for me. I'm doing it because this is what I like doing. I don't have any expectations of success anymore; I'm here because this meal with these people is a lot more fun than watching TV or going bowling."

By now everyone had taken their chance to speak, and we all looked strangely at peace with what had been said. I thanked everyone for sharing their authentic emotions. I said, "With the exception of our wonderful, positive Shelly, what I heard people saying is that hope is not about outcome, but about process. Hope is the energy created in the process of acting as if we were hopeful."

After the legislative vote of the day, we were indeed a sadder group, but wiser, chastened by our realization that power is entrenched and skilled. We had learned that every victory comes with an asterisk. There was always a loophole that allowed the XL pipeline to move forward. But we had also realized that defeats come with asterisks, too. Within every defeat, we could find a way to keep protecting what we loved.

Ken had the last word about what had happened at the capitol that day. He said, "This fight isn't over until we give up. And we are *never* giving up!"

Creating Joy

On May 5, our group gathered at the observatory to connect our Lincoln dot with dots all over the world. We had the treats our group promised to bring, wonderful young musicians, face painting, and a teenage volunteer from the zoo who brought a butterscotch-colored hedgehog for children to hold. It was ninety-five degrees, which in itself was a statement. Fortunately, there was just enough shade for the hundred or so people who showed up for our event.

Joel Sartore spoke first. He had returned at one a.m. the night before from a two-week photo shoot and needed to rush off to his son's soccer game. But he wanted to thank our group for its work on stopping the pipeline and to reinforce the idea that small groups like ours would be the change agents for the world.

Ken spoke next. He had brought all of his children to the event, and he introduced them to the group. He explained how, all over the world, small groups of people just like us were getting together to talk about climate- and weather-related issues in their particular places, and to share this information with everyone else in the world who was interested.

Ken explained that our particular statement on 350.org's Connect the Climate Dots web page would say, "Spring came to Nebraska a month early this year." And indeed, already the peonies, which usually bloom in Nebraska around Memorial Day, were in full bloom, and the cilantro—which is our first crop for farmers' market—had gone to seed before the market even opened.

Duane, from the Nebraska Wildlife Federation, talked to us about energy. He stated that our power district was at a crossroads and must make decisions about investing in coal or in alternative energy sources. He handed out materials and suggested ways we could influence the decision process.

Shelly left her Dippin' Dots stand to read a poem about Thai bees from her book *The Cockroach Monologues*. This particular species of bee survives by drinking human tears. After her poem, she encouraged everyone to help themselves to free ice cream.

The last speaker was Ken's daughter Helen, now fifteen. Her long blond hair whipped in the wind as she spoke with passion about the world she wanted to live in and the world she was willing to create. Her sincerity and fervor gave all of us hope for the future.

After Helen's remarks, all of us gathered together and followed Wesaam to a spot for our photo. We held up an eight-foot-wide black dot and assembled around it. Wesaam took several pictures of our Lincoln group to beam around the world. Then we returned to the shade to drink lemonade and listen to music.

In the end, the afternoon reminded me of the church picnics of my girlhood. We watched the children play, talked about summer plans, and chatted about each other's lives. We didn't have a victory against TransCanada, but we had an important victory as individuals in a group. We had found each other and kept ourselves sane and reasonably happy in a difficult time. By acting as if we had hope, we created hope for ourselves; by acting as if we had power, we felt a sense of control over our own fates.

Of course, our coalition was not just about our own mental health. It was about protecting our state and saving our planet. Yet almost all truly great causes—world peace, the abolition of slavery, the eradication of hunger—offer no quick victories.

My aunt Grace often said, "I get what I want because I know what to want." Her wise remark applies here. By our actions, we realistically want to experience joy and a connection to other people. The coalition gave us these things as well as the motivation, energy, and ideas to continue working hard to stop the pipeline. Nobody knows at this moment whether or not there will be a pipeline across our state. So we will keep working. But we do know that in the years ahead, we have a beloved community to support us in all ways.

TWELVE

The Rolling Waves

Hope as a Process

*On we go—with just enough surprises in the
world to keep me from going dark.*

BILL MCKIBBEN

I began this book after reading *Eaarth* and during a time
when it looked like TransCanada would succeed in building
a pipeline that could destroy my state's water supply. I felt
traumatized by what I knew and uncertain about how to turn
my anguish and anger into anything positive for either myself
or other people. In other words, I felt spiritually shipwrecked.

But after a while, I managed to organize myself emotionally and go to work. With a few other people, I formed a small
group and we began a journey of discovery. At first we were
pessimistic about our chances of success. But somehow in
the midst of vegetarian potlucks and Pumpkins Against the
Pipeline parties, we began to feel empowered, connected, and
courageous. And by the end, we loved each other.

As I write this today, I don't know what will happen with

the tar sands, but I do know what has happened to me. Writing this book has been my own voyage from trauma to transcendence. I have found my people, the ones nearby who care about protecting our state as much as I do. And I have discovered a process that keeps me emotionally healthy and actively enjoying my life.

I have learned that reviving the planet and reviving ourselves are not opposed, but rather deeply congruent behaviors. Fixing inner and outer space are the same process. We can't heal ourselves without healing our environments, and we can't be mentally healthy when the green boat is sinking and we are pretending the trauma isn't happening. As the Great Acceleration occurs, unless we are part of the Great Turning, we will drown in the global storms.

Of course, my action doesn't always keep my despair at bay. But my engagement in and love of the world give me perspective. For every great tragedy occurring or looming on the horizon, I know how to make an action plan. I have a sense for how to access the sparkling moment. And I know how to step outdoors and look for the green heron or the redolent milkweed blossom.

Most days it is difficult to find any evidence of changes that are even close to the scale we need to see. However, most days it's also easy to find evidence of positive change: a helpful new law, a sustainability group forming, an effective piece of investigative journalism, or a victory for a particular place or animal species. Usually I am optimistic on days I go to the farmers' market and pessimistic when I read about our political discourse on global problems. Sometimes I feel as if ignorance and greed are insurmountable; then I interact with others who are fiercely devoted to a sustainable future and I rally. In a sense, there is no such thing as false hope. Hope creates new realities.

I try not to be too caught up in my fluctuating emotions and I especially don't predict the future. I know it will not be at all like the past. To quote John Gorka, "Our old future is gone."

I also try not to evaluate myself in terms of the results of my actions. Rather, I focus on the quality of my interactions and the joy I feel every day. Joanna Macy, when asked about her own life, responded, "No great assessments." I try to follow her wise suggestion and take things a day at a time.

We are all in process, unfolding, unfurling into each other. Everything that is happening to me is happening to you and many things that are happening to us are happening to the manatees and to the bees, too.

We are tumbling through time like shells on a breaking wave. On what shore we will land, we do not know. We cannot go backward in time; we can only go forward.

The truth is we simply don't know what time it is. We cannot see our place in the homo sapiens timeline. Maybe we are in the last generation. Or maybe we are in the first generation of a great turning toward wholeness and vibrancy.

Former Czech president Václav Havel wrote of a moment in time when societies come to their senses and decide to live "outside the lie." That happened in his country, the Czech Republic, and he believed it could happen anywhere.

Right now, many of us feel like Havel felt when he lived in a deluded country. We can feel crushed by all the mistakes and lies around us. Yet all over the world, people like us are organizing themselves and their communities for positive change. When we do this, we not only emerge from our own trance, but we begin a process of breaking the trance of our culture. There is no finer cause.

I can sense the tide turning in our country. The Occupy movement is a good example of people coming out of their trances and working together to build a new kind of world. Locally and nationally, people are becoming more engaged and connected to their communities.

Democracy may yet be reborn as this next generation redefines it in the context of our corrupt and oligarchic times. In fact, our present moment reminds me of the 1960s, with the great injustices of segregation and the Vietnam War. Young people became activists because they were desperate, and collective despair can energize citizens. In our current situation, the young adults in our country are our greatest resource. If our many global challenges have a bright side, young adults are that bright side.

The fresh breezes of honesty and engagement are helping us sail out of a Sargasso Sea. What we are seeing is not really a revolution but an evolution, a transformation in the way we think about our relationships to each other and all living beings. More and more of us are grasping that we are all connected and part of one living organism, our biosphere. Yet oddly this new consciousness is similar to an ancient idea. Was not Eden a verdant, fruited place where humans and animals lived together in peace and joy? And in fact, were not all the ancestral homes of all peoples places of harmony and beauty?

The big surprise is not that humans are destroying the

earth. That has been going on for quite a while. What is new and heartening is our awareness and action on behalf of the earth. Entrepreneur Paul Hawken estimates that there are two million groups worldwide working for environmental change, social and economic justice, and indigenous peoples' rights. Many more people would work if they believed that changes were possible and their efforts mattered. As we join the millions of people who are working for a sustainable planet, we won't be sacrificing, but rather building new lives based on our deep true selves.

Nobody knows what will happen to the planet, but we do know what makes humans stronger, healthier, and more resilient. That is facing the truth, dealing with it emotionally, and transforming it. Regardless of the results of our work, when we are doing our best, we feel happier and less alone. With the right attitude, we can withstand any storm.

Many living species have traveled across time with us, and we want to believe this journey of all living creatures will extend far into the distant future. Every being that is alive today shares this same long history, going back to LUCA. We don't want our chains of DNA to be broken in the next one hundred years, or ever. We all want to be links to a long future.

Humanity is facing a crucial decade. Our individual and cultural resilience systems will be fully tested and elucidated. At this moment in time we have the opportunity to work together for the right to a future for our children and the children of all living species, and for the right to a healthy, sustainable planet. This is our only world, after all.

Happiness and sustainability depend on everyone healing everyone else. As we repair our relationships with the web of life, the web of life will repair us. Healing the earth is not a liberal or conservative idea—it is a form of prayer.

The Green Boat

This book's title, *The Green Boat*, comes from the name my husband Jim and I gave our boat-shaped piece of land. Our house sits atop a dam that overlooks a city park. From our deck, we can watch the sun and moon rise over the lake. Great storms roll in from the south and west and explode over us as they move toward the Missouri River.

The ducks, geese, and pelicans come through in the fall and spring. In the summer a great blue heron couple nests in the reeds at the south end of the lake. When I work in the garden, I hear the songs of meadowlarks and kingbirds. Bikers and hikers use the trails and fishermen catch perch and bluegill. On weekends, parades of kayaks, sailboats, and canoes crisscross the lake.

On snowy nights, a red fox comes to hunt on our dam. He looks as if he is dancing. In the winter, we watch as children sled on the dam and skate and play hockey on the lake. In their bright coats, they resemble confetti swirling on soft white frosting. At night, from the warmth of our living room, we observe the ice fishermen with their insulated clothing, tiny-lighted huts, and bottles of whiskey.

The Green Boat is a small but rich ecosystem that gives us great joy. We know how lucky we are to live here. Jim and I try to share this good place with others so that it is not just our Green Boat, but rather it is the communal property of everyone.

We share what Martin Luther King Jr. called "the inescapable network of mutuality." If a bird dies here, we bury him. When our friends need a quiet, green place to relax, we invite them here. If it is time for a celebration, what better place than under the Nebraska sky surrounded by trees and water?

Most of us take care of what we love and we grow to love what we take care of. Every place has the potential to be beautiful and filled with love—in other words, sacred. Our blue, gold, and green planet is indeed a Noah's Ark of sorts with over seven billion people and billions more plants and animals. If we don't sail carefully and tend to those on board, we will perish. If we manage to keep our boat afloat, our world can sail on, not as it is today, but in a more joyous, peaceful, and beautiful way.

ACKNOWLEDGMENTS

To my readers—Pam Barger; Louise Dunlap; Jane Isay; Lynda Madison; Bill McKibben; Jim and Jamie Pipher; and Stephanie Sugars.

To my webmasters, John Gilliam and Scot Adams.

To my author page manager, Sara Gilliam.

To Jeremy Johnson for his inspiring art.

To Helen Winston for permission to use her speech.

To Aubrey Streit Krug, my trusty first mate.

To Reynold Peterson for his wonderful cover art.

To the people I interviewed—Pete Beyers and Deepa Gupta, Chris Blake, Jenny Bruning Brown, Meghan Davidson, George and Sherri Hanigan, Marian Langan, Joel Sartore, Sarah Kramer, Brad Kindler, Deb Hauswald, George and Sherri Hanigan, Adam Hintz, Tiffany Hogan, Paul Olson, Mitch Paine, Jamie Pipher, Suzy Prenger, Tim Rinne, Chris and Vicki Sommerich, Ian Tattersol, and Dave and Monique Tilford.

To the members of our coalition—Wesaam Al-Baldry, John Atkeison, M. J. Berry, Buffalo Bruce, Graham Christensen, Shelly

Clark-Geiser, Malinda Frevert, Ben Gotschall, Christy and Richard Hargesheimer, Adam Hintz, Duane Hovorka, Mohamed Jollah, Chelsea Johnson, Jane Kleeb, Brad Kindler, Marian Langan, Nancy Packard, Mitch Paine, Tim Rinne, Marge Saiser, Carol Smith, Larry Weixelman, Pippa White, Ken Winston, and T. Marni Vos.

To Susan Lee Cohen, whose advice has been sage, heartfelt, and spot-on. She helped launch this book and bring it into a safe harbor.

To Jake Morrissey, my true friend and the best navigator on the seas.

To Craig Burke, Marilyn Ducksworth, Geoff Kloske, Susan Petersen Kennedy, and all of my other shipmates at Penguin USA.

To my son, Zeke, my sister Jane Oh-Dang-Go Bray, and my grandchildren, Kate, Aidan, Claire, and Coltrane.

To Jim, my cocaptain.

SUGGESTED READING

Abram, David. *The Spell of the Sensuous: Perception and Language in a More-Than-Human World*. Vintage Books, 1996.

Avery, Samuel. *The Pipeline and the Paradigm: Keystone XL, Tar Sands, and the Battle to Defuse the Carbon Bomb*. Ruka Press, 2013.

Brown, Lester R. *Plan B 4.0: Mobilizing to Save Civilization*. W. W. Norton, 2009.

———. *World on the Edge: How to Prevent Environmental and Economic Collapse*. W. W. Norton, 2011.

Cohen, Stanley. *States of Denial: Knowing About Atrocities and Suffering*. Polity, 2001.

Diamond, Jared. *Collapse: How Societies Choose to Fail or Succeed*. Viking, 2005.

Eiseley, Loren. *The Immense Journey: An Imaginative Naturalist Explores the Mysteries of Man and Nature*. Vintage, 1959.

Gessner, David. *My Green Manifesto: Down the Charles River in Pursuit of a New Environmentalism*. Milkweed Editions, 2011.

Hansen, James. *Storms of My Grandchildren: The Truth About the Coming Climate Catastrophe and Our Last Chance to Save Humanity*. Bloomsbury USA, 2009.

Hawken, Paul. *Blessed Unrest: How the Largest Social Movement in His-

tory Is Restoring Grace, Justice, and Beauty to the World. Penguin, 2008.

Hertsgaard, Mark. *Hot: Living Through the Next Fifty Years on Earth.* Mariner Books, 2012.

Hochschild, Adam. *Bury the Chains: Prophets and Rebels in the Fight to Free an Empire's Slaves.* Mariner, 2006.

Hoose, Phillip H., Hannah Hoose, and Deb Tilley. *Hey, Little Ant.* Random House, 1998.

Hopkins, Rob. *The Transition Handbook: From Oil Dependency to Local Resilience.* Chelsea Green, 2008.

Intergovernmental Panel on Climate Change. *Fourth Assessment Report: Climate Change 2007.* http://www.ipcc.ch/publications_and_data /ar4/syr/en/contents.html.

Keogh, Martin, ed. *Hope Beneath Our Feet: Restoring Our Place in the Natural World.* North Atlantic Books, 2010.

Kolbert, Elizabeth. *Field Notes from a Catastrophe: Man, Nature, and Climate Change.* Bloomsbury, 2006.

Macy, Joanna, and Chris Johnstone. *Active Hope: How to Face the Mess We're in Without Going Crazy.* New World Library, 2012.

Macy, Joanna, and Molly Young Brown. *Coming Back to Life: Practices to Reconnect Our Lives, Our World.* New Society Publishers, 1998.

Meadows, Donella H., Dennis L. Meadows, and Jørgen Randers. *Beyond the Limits: Confronting Global Collapse, Envisioning a Sustainable Future.* Chelsea Green, 1993.

McKibben, Bill. *The Age of Missing Information.* Random House, 2006.
———. *Eaarth: Making a Life on a Tough New Planet.* St. Martin's Griffin, 2011.

Neihardt, John G. *Black Elk Speaks: Being the Life Story of a Holy Man of the Oglala Sioux.* State University of New York Press, 2008.

Nhat Hanh, Thich. *The World We Have: A Buddhist Approach to Peace and Ecology.* Parallax Press, 2008.

Patel, Raj. *The Value of Nothing: How to Reshape Market Society and Redefine Democracy.* Picador, 2010.

Quinn, Daniel. *Ishmael: An Adventure of the Mind and Spirit.* Bantam, 1995.

Rifkin, Jeremy. *The Empathic Civilization: The Race to Global Consciousness in a World in Crisis.* Tarcher, 2009.

Ruppert, Michael C. *Confronting Collapse: The Crisis of Energy and Money in a Post Peak Oil World*. Chelsea Green, 2009.

Russell, Peter. *The Global Brain: An Awakening Earth in a New Century*. Floris Books, 2007.

Solnit, Rebecca. *A Paradise Built in Hell: The Extraordinary Communities That Arise in Disaster*. Viking, 2009.

Taylor, Betsy. *More Fun, Less Stuff Starter Kit*. Center for a New American Dream, 2001.

Williams, Terry Tempest. "The Gulf Between Us" in *Orion* Nov./Dec. 2010. http://www.orionmagazine.org/index.php/articles/article/5931.

INDEX

In each of her groundbreaking books, therapist and bestselling author **Mary Pipher, Ph.D.,** shows us how to see life's challenges through a very human lens.

Whether it's the problems faced by adolescent girls, or families, or older loved ones, Pipher uses her keen powers of observation and her deep understanding of human nature to reveal that each of us holds the solutions to many of the troubles we face. We just need to look within.

© Angela Zegers

The classic on girls' adolescence

A clear and perceptive call to reexamine the plight of adolescent girls as they face the daunting pressures society throws at them today—at an age when many of them aren't developmentally or emotionally equipped to handle them.

"An important book...Pipher shines high-beam headlights on the world of teenage girls."

—Los Angeles Times

"A must-read for all of us who care about young women in our lives... *Reviving Ophelia* arms us with information we can use in helping our daughters grow to adulthood with their strength intact."

—Lincoln Journal Star

A compassionate primer on family

In *The Shelter of Each Other*, Mary Pipher opens our eyes to the complicated realities that families everywhere face, and she shows us a way forward. She clears a path to the strength and energy that lie at the core of family life. Wise and impassioned, this book challenges us to find the courage to protect and nurture the families that we cherish.

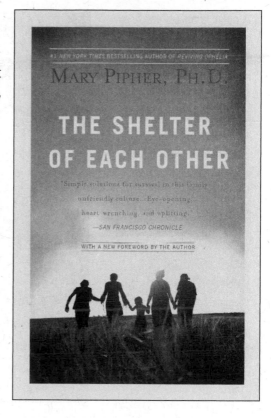

"A canny mix of optimism and practicality gives Pipher's fans a way to resist the worst of the culture around them and substitute the best of themselves."

—Newsweek

"Eye-opening...Pipher's simple solutions for survival in this family-unfriendly culture are peppered through with the heart-wrenching and uplifting stories of several of her clients' families."

—San Francisco Chronicle

A hopeful, helpful guide to aging

As our loved ones grow older, it's difficult to find the words to talk about the challenges they face. We need new maps to navigate between generations. *Another Country* is a field guide to this foreign landscape—both a help and a resource. With realism and respect, Mary Pipher gets inside the minds, hearts, and bodies of older people and helps us to understand the geography of aging.

"Pipher explores how today's mobile, individualistic, media-drenched culture prevents so many dependent old people, and the relatives trying to do right by them, from getting what they need....Her insights will help people of several generations." **—The Washington Post**

"Totally accessible...A compassionate...look at the disconnect between baby boomers and their aging parents or grandparents." **—USA Today**

T277-0413

An inspirational guide for change

Writing to Change the World is a powerfully instructive manual for those who seek to effect social change with nothing but their message and a keyboard. Combining practical instruction with rousing commentary, Pipher spurs readers to ensure that their messages touch readers: shaking their beliefs, expanding their perspectives, and even changing the world.

"[Pipher] offers useful advice....[This] will encourage idealistic aspiring writers, who will surely find happiness in her assertion that writing can change the world." —*Publishers Weekly*

"[Pipher] brings astute analogies from her career as a therapist to the problem of how to begin writing." —*Library Journal*

T278-0413

Mary Pipher's moving personal story

In *Seeking Peace*, therapist and bestselling author Mary Pipher turns her attention inward, exploring the lessons of her own life: as a daughter, a mother, a wife, a therapist, and a seeker. In the process she reveals what she learned in her—and by extension our—search for happiness and love.

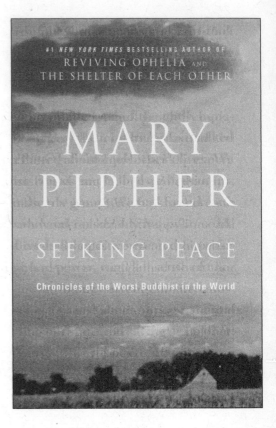

"Pipher's account...is hard to put down with its smooth, compact, and insightful prose....[An] absorbing chronicle of discovery." **—Booklist**

T279-0413